The

Richard Cocl
researchers
presentation and analysis of data.

Dr Cocks is an operational research consultant with eight years' experience in the Treasury and other government departments, currently working in the water industry. Dr Bentley has worked as a financial analyst in the oil industry and is currently a Senior Research Fellow in the University of Reading's Cybernetics Department.

£300 Billion

Government Spending:

The Facts

Richard Cocks and Roger Bentley

Databooks

Published in Great Britain by
Databooks, 11 Cutbush Close, Lower Earley, Reading, RG6 4XA

British Library Cataloguing in Publication Data

ISBN 0 9527688 0 1

Designed and Typeset by Snap Creative, Reading, Berkshire
Printed and bound in Great Britain by Cox and Wyman,
Reading, Berkshire

Although a great deal of effort has gone into compiling this book the authors
can accept no responsibility for the accuracy of the data included.

Contents

When I was working in the Treasury I felt privileged to have easy access to details of government spending, while outside I knew that friends - intelligent and otherwise well-informed people - had little idea of where their money was going. Clearly something was wrong, and so the idea for this book was born.

Several years later I met Roger Bentley, who had been thinking along somewhat similar lines, and we decided to produce together a booklet that would summarise government spending, as visually as possible. Pictures can show so much, if well chosen, so we began by simply producing pie charts, and envisaged a much slimmer guide. But we found ourselves presenting numbers for spending that we did not ourselves understand, so explanations were needed and the book rapidly grew to its present size.

We hope that in this form it will be useful to people with quite specific interests and information needs, as well as to the thoughtful layman for whom it was first intended.

We would welcome any comments on our coverage and presentation, and suggestions for future editions. Please contact us either through the publisher's address or directly by e-mail at: R.W.Bentley@reading.ac.uk.

R.J.C.
July 1996.

Acknowledgements

The encouragement of many people has been invaluable in maintaining our commitment to this book, but we must single out Margaret and the rest of the Cocks family, without whose support and forbearance we would have given up long ago. We also want to warmly thank the numerous civil servants who have helped us, both professionally and through their personal interest. In particular we thank Helen Brown and colleagues at the Treasury who patiently responded to a steady stream of questions and requests.

We would like to dedicate this book to the thousands of public servants who actually carry out the work described and costed in these pages, and whose own dedication is one of the strengths of our democracy.

'Open government is a part of effective democracy. Citizens must have adequate access to information and analysis on which government business is based.'
- The 1993 White Paper on Open Government

The aim of this book is to provide a comprehensive picture of government spending.

When we hear about the amount of money spent on a new government scheme, or the cost of making a particular tax cut, most of us don't have any way of putting it into perspective. Unless we are used to dealing in large numbers, we simply register anything above a few million pounds as 'a large amount of money'.

So in this book we try to help the reader gain a feeling for the numbers involved. This starts with the book's title, as £300 billion is roughly what the government spends in total each year - about £5,000 per person. We then describe how this money is allocated. If, at the end of the book, you know that roughly £100 billion goes to Social Security, £40 billion to Health and £20 billion to Defence, you will have a better feeling for government spending than most.

We deal with government spending for the whole of the UK. Local as well as central government spending is covered and, while not every programme is shown in detail, all the money the government spends is included somewhere on the main pie charts, so that a solid picture of 'what goes where' can emerge.

We have focused on government spending forecasts for the current year, 1996-97[1], because although some spending will differ from these estimates we believe it is more useful to show them, and discuss the current issues that surround them, than to present historical figures.

Most of the data in this book are drawn directly from Departmental reports, pulled together with the help of Treasury publications and advice. For a brief description of the methods and assumptions used, see the Annex: Methodology and Notes.

---

1   1996-97 refers to the year from April 1st 1996 to March 31st 1997.

Despite new policy initiatives, efficiency savings, 'cuts' and reorganisations, government spending on most of its programmes - particularly the larger ones - cannot change substantially over the short term. The complex systems involved and, more importantly, the needs that they address, have considerable inertia so although the pattern of spending below is taken from the government's plans for 1996-97 (used as the reference year throughout this book), it will not change by very much over the next few years. (For a view of the changes that have occurred over a somewhat longer timespan, see Chapter 19.)

General Government Spending
1996-97: £307 billion

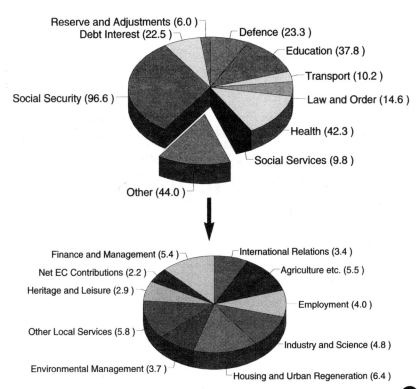

Reserve and Adjustments (6.0)
Debt Interest (22.5)
Defence (23.3)
Education (37.8)
Transport (10.2)
Social Security (96.6)
Law and Order (14.6)
Health (42.3)
Social Services (9.8)
Other (44.0)

Finance and Management (5.4)
International Relations (3.4)
Net EC Contributions (2.2)
Agriculture etc. (5.5)
Heritage and Leisure (2.9)
Employment (4.0)
Other Local Services (5.8)
Industry and Science (4.8)
Environmental Management (3.7)
Housing and Urban Regeneration (6.4)

Trends in Total Spending

Government spending is increasing every year. And in most years it also increases after the effect of inflation has been taken into account. This occurs largely because of the increase in the real wealth of society, which is reflected in public spending through the wages paid to public servants, and in the standards expected for education and health care provision etc..

To adjust for the increasing level of wealth of the country as a whole, usually measured as Gross Domestic Product (GDP), we can look at government spending in terms of its ratio to this. The following chart shows both the inflation-adjusted expenditure and its ratio to the prevailing GDP:

General Government Expenditure

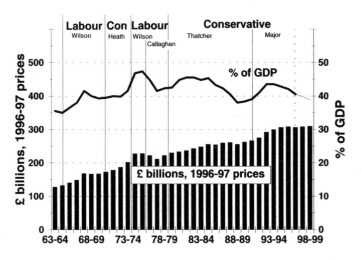

While there is a more or less steady rise in 'real' government spending, the ratio to GDP shows no long-term trend, despite substantial fluctuations. We have added details of the political parties in power, because of the link frequently made between particular parties and the tendency for public spending to expand or contract.

The government has a target of reducing the percentage to 40 per cent, and hopes to achieve this by 1997-98.

Definitions

Government expenditure can be expressed in various ways depending on
how one treats items like privatisation proceeds, Lottery spending and
interest receipts. The definition of expenditure used above, and
throughout this book, is the Treasury's 'GGE(X)'. GGE stands for
General Government Expenditure, covering local as well as central
government. The 'X' means that it excludes:

• interest and dividend receipts - these are netted off gross debt interest;

• Lottery-financed spending and

• privatisation proceeds (which are regarded as negative spending under
   the other main, broader, definition of GGE used by the government).

When the National Lottery first started, its proceeds were included in
GGE(X), but then later removed. This seems preferable, as the Lottery
has been promoted as providing new money rather than substituting for
government funding. It also helps keep down the ratio of GGE(X) to
GDP.

A minor difference between our figures and the government's arises
because we do not deduct the £0.6 billion income from the sale of
housing corporations' loans portfolios (see Chapter 8), treating it in the
same way as other privatisation proceeds. The government treats it as
negative spending within its definition of GGE(X).

Note that government grants and loans to public corporations and
nationalised industries are included in GGE(X), but their spending
financed from other borrowing or from revenue is not.

Definitions

Central and Local Government Spending

In the pie charts, as in most of this book, we look at general government spending
as a whole, rather than separating central from local spending. There are two
reasons for this.

Firstly, there is nothing absolute about the division. The last fifteen years have seen
major changes in the methods by which much of the public sector is funded. Many
schools and all polytechnics, for example, have moved out of the local authority
sector and are now funded directly from central government departments, or

indirectly via funding councils. The sourcing of funds for different services thus varies from time to time for pragmatic or political reasons.

Secondly, central government dictates to a very large degree how much money the local authorities have available, and how they must spend it. It provides most of their income, and caps their overall budgets to just below £75 billion - a level consistent with its plans for the overall level of public spending.

The final sections of this chapter look at the government's approach to current and capital spending in the public sector.

Central Government Running Costs

The cost of employing, accommodating and equipping the 500,000 or so civil servants, across all departments and programmes, is £14.8 billion. Although this represents only about 7 per cent of central government's total spending it is seen as a key area in which savings should be made. By 1998-99 the government wants the total down to £14.3 billion - a reduction of 8.5 per cent in real terms over the two years.

A key element of the drive to force down costs has been the designation of many parts of government as *Next Steps* Agencies (from the 1988 report *Improving Management in Government: the Next Steps*). These are separate business units each with its own Chief Executive, well-defined objectives and a framework document formally setting out its relationships with other parts of government. As well as traditionally separately identifiable bodies, such as the Royal Mint and the Insolvency Service, they include numerous sub-departmental units, for example the 27 Executive Offices within the Inland Revenue. Three quarters of all civil servants now work in agencies and units run on these lines.

For many agencies, like the Meteorological Office, the next 'next step' is then Trading Fund status, with the government buying back its services.

The Private Finance Initiative (PFI)

As well as encouraging the movement of many of its traditional functions towards the private sector, the government is looking to replace public spending on major capital schemes by private investment. This new approach to financing public works is being overseen by the Private Finance Panel. By the end of 1995 it had identified over 1,000 schemes, worth £25 billion, as potential candidates for private finance.

£5 billion worth had been agreed by March 1996 and a similar volume are expected to have been signed-up by the end of 1996-97. But actual private spending during the year is expected to be only about £1.9 billion. This is much lower than the £3.7 billion fall-off in government-funded capital investment, because many projects which would now be under way have been delayed for investigation of the PFI option.

Current PFI investment is dominated by transport schemes and in particular the Channel Tunnel Rail Link, for which the total private finance will be around £2.7 billion. Amongst other projects already in progress, financed by investors who will later charge the public sector for their use, are the Bridgend and Fazakerley prisons (£100 million total), a new medical university in London (£100 million) and the South Buckinghamshire NHS Trust rebuild (£35 million).

Local authorities also are being encouraged to use private finance, by the cutting of their grants for capital spending - down by 16 per cent (in real terms) on two years ago - and the relaxing of the rules which previously limited their freedom to use private sector funding.

In the short-term, government spending is reduced through avoiding much direct capital investment; in future years current spending will be increased to cover costs - plus profit - over the assets' lifespans. So the net consequences for the public purse depend on whether or not the profit that the investors will make is offset by the hoped-for efficiencies in construction costs brought about by use of competitive tendering and private sector disciplines.

Further Information

Public Expenditure Statistical Analysis 1996-97, HM Treasury, 1996. Cm 3201, HMSO.

Financial Statement and Budget Report, HM Treasury. November 1995. HC 30, HMSO.

To adapt to the new political map, defence forces around the world have been reviewing and restructuring. Britain set itself a target of achieving a 16 per cent reduction in its defence spending over the six years from 1990/91 to 1996/97, with other NATO countries making similar plans. The 1990 "Options for Change" defence review began the process here by making substantial cuts, mainly in the army. This was followed in July 1993 by a white paper proposing major cuts in the Royal Navy, in particular the forces that previously defended the Atlantic shipping lanes, and in July 1994 by the "Front-Line First" recommendations of further reductions.

Defence 1996-97
£ 23.3 billion

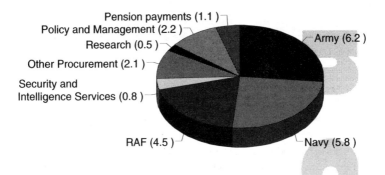

Pension payments (1.1)
Policy and Management (2.2)
Research (0.5)
Other Procurement (2.1)
Security and Intelligence Services (0.8)
RAF (4.5)
Army (6.2)
Navy (5.8)

During the 1980s there were large changes in the level of real-terms spending, with substantial growth followed by a general downward trend from 1984.

Defence Expenditure Trend
1996-97 Prices

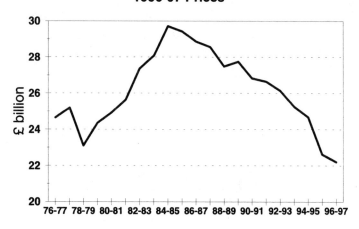

The cost reduction achieved since 1990 has been over 20 per cent, comfortably exceeding the 16 per cent originally sought.

In the sections below dealing with the three main services, their expenditure is shown broken down into three categories: operational costs, mainly for personnel and consumables; the costs of logistical support of in-service equipment - its storage, supply, repair and maintenance; and procurement costs for the development and production of new equipment, dominated by ships, tanks and aircraft.

The Army

Army, 1996-97

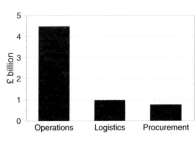

Total army manpower is about 109,000, in some 95 regiments, with another 59,000 men in the Territorial Army. The numbers of professionals are down from around 170,000 in 1980. Ironically, since the recent redundancy programmes of the early '90s recruitment has become a problem, and the army is about 4,000 men below strength.

Major Army Equipment[1]

449	Challenger tanks
243	Other tanks
782 [2]	Warrior armoured combat vehicles
2993 [2]	Saxon armoured personnel carriers and Scimitar armoured combat vehicles
63	Multiple Launch Rocket Systems
468	Other artillery
52	Armoured Vehicle Launched Bridges
279	Helicopters

1   As at November 1995.
2   Under the Conventional Armed Forces in Europe Treaty, more than 1000 of these armoured combat vehicles are precluded from carrying an infantry section, and so limited in their capability.

The largest current procurement programme is for 350 Vickers Challenger 2 tanks to replace more of the old Chieftains. Also, two orders have recently been given to Land Rover: one for 8,000 light and medium utility trucks to replace the current vehicles and the second a £60 million order for 800 field ambulances - modified Discoveries.

The main spending on new equipment over the next few years will on 67 McDonnell-Douglas Apache "tankbusting" attack helicopters at about £35 million each, to replace the Lynx. The American parts are being assembled in Yeovil by Westland - so the helicopter will be known as the Westland

Apache - and a number of components will also be provided by British suppliers, including the £1 million pair of Rolls-Royce engines for each aircraft. Once delivered to the army, in the year 2000, they will have an operational life of about 30 years.

Britain's Contribution to UN Operations

The Foreign Office is very keen to maintain Britain's position as a permanent member of the UN Security Council, and to do so we must be seen to be ready to provide forces for peacekeeping, as we have done in Bosnia. It is the Foreign Office budget that pays the running costs of peacekeeping operations, costing £275 million in 1995-96, although the UN would like to see it as an integral part of each nation's defence budget.

During 1995-96 we contributed 8,000 troops to UNPROFOR in the former Yugoslavia, and were at one point the largest contributor to the humanitarian relief operation. In the air, our aircraft played a substantial part in the patrol, reconnaissance and bombing missions against Serb targets, as well as flying in 27,000 tonnes of aid to Sarajevo during its four-year seige.

All three aircraft carriers were deployed to the Adriatic in support of UN operations, with their Sea Harriers flying over 1,700 sorties.

At the start of 1996-97, 10,500 British military personnel were contributing to the UN's Peace Implementation Force, IFOR, itself commanded by a British Lieutenant General. We are also contributing 28 helicopters and nine Harrier GR7s for a variety of roles.

On another continent, following the 1995 ceasefire in the 20-year Angolan civil war, the UN asked Britain to set up a logistics infrastructure for its Angola Verification Mission, UNAVEM III. In three months, the 650 men of the Logistics Battalion Group set up a supply system for the peacekeepers and restored treated water supplies to over a million people.

Our commitment to support UN peacekeping operations is one reason why we justify spending more per capita on defence than most other countries - 2.8 per cent of GDP compared with the average of 2.3 per cent for our NATO European allies. The difference costs us nearly £4 billion a year.

Britain's Contribution to UN Operations

The Royal Navy

Navy, 1996-97

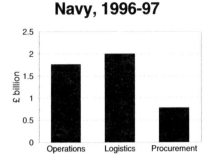

Naval manpower of 50,000 is being reduced by about 2,000 during 1996-97 through a redundancy programme, while recruitment to junior ranks is, like the army, failing to meet targets. The main shortfall is in the Royal Marines. Full-time servicemen are supplemented by 4,000 Volunteer Reserves.

Nuclear Weapons

Britain's strategic nuclear capability consists of two Vanguard Class submarines, HMS *Vanguard* and HMS *Victorious*, carrying Trident D5 ballistic missiles. The last two Polaris submarines, HMS *Repulse* and HMS *Renown*, are being decommissioned during 1996 - earlier than planned due to problems with their nuclear propulsion systems.

A third Vanguard submarine, HMS *Vigilant*, comes into service in 1998 and the fourth, HMS *Vengeance* around the year 2000. The total cost of the Trident programme is estimated at £12 billion, at current prices.

Each submarine can carry sixteen missiles, each weighing 60 tonnes and with up to twelve UK-built Multiple Independent Re-Entry Vehicle warheads (MIRVs) on its US-built rocket. But this level of firepower is now something of an embarrassment, and we have committed ourselves to carry a maximum of only 96 warheads on each submarine.

Until HMS *Vigilant* comes into service we are also maintaining a separate sub-strategic nuclear capability. This is the WE177, a simple free-fall bomb dropped by Tornados.

By the turn of the century Britain's megatonnage will be about 40 per cent of the 1970's level, and about 10 per cent of the nuclear capability available to the US or Russia after their implementation of the START II reductions.

'Nuclear Weapons'

Major Naval Equipment[1]

	Type	Principal function
Ships:		
12	Destroyers	Area air defence
24	Frigates	Anti-submarine
2	Trident submarines	Nuclear missile carriers
12	Fleet submarines	Attack (nuclear powered)
3	Aircraft carriers	Anti-submarine
18	Minehunters /minesweepers	Clearing mines
5	Landing ships	Troop Landing
8	Patrol	Offshore patrol
48	Other	Patrol, training, survey, supply, repair
Aircraft:		
22	Sea Harriers	Defence, attack and reconnaissance
4	Harriers	Defence, attack and reconnaissance
45	Sea Kings	Anti-submarine
43	Sea Kings	Early warning, assault, search and rescue
49	Lynx	Anti-submarine / anti-ship
6	Lynx	Commando assault
9	Gazelle	Commando assault
17	Gazelle	Training
12	Hawk	Training and support
11	Jetstreams	Training and support

1 As at 1 April 1996.

The main ship losses due to restructuring have been a reduction of eleven in the number of destroyers and frigates since 1993. And all conventionally-fuelled and some nuclear-powered submarines have been decommissioned. By contrast, the fleet of mine countermeasures vessels is being increased, with an order for a further seven Sandown class minehunters.

Other ships being built include a final six Duke Class Type 23 frigates, to replace older Type 22s at a cost of about £150 million each, and the navy's first helicopter carrier, HMS Oceon, which is planned to come into service in 1998.

An order for up to five more £500 million Trafalgar hunter-killer nuclear submarines has recently been placed with GEC, to replace the existing Swiftsure vessels around the year 2004. In the mean time the Swiftsures are being upgraded.

With respect to aircraft, 44 EH101 Merlin helicopters and 16 more Sea Harriers are on order, while a mid-life update programme to bring the 35 older Sea Harriers up to the same F/A2 standard is nearly complete.

The largest weapons purchase planned is for 65 conventionally-armed Tomahawk land attack cruise missiles, for fitting to the fleet submarines. These will cost about £650 million.

Support facilities are being substantially rationalised. The Portland Naval Base and the Maritime Headquarters at Pitreavie are being closed and Rosyth Naval Base downgraded to a Royal Navy Support Establishment. Invitations to tender are being issued to undertake the refitting work currently carried out by the Fleet Maintenance and Repair Organisation at Plymouth. Negotiations are also under way to sell the Devonport and Rosyth Royal Dockyards - although work is in progress to provide Devonport with facilities for refitting the Trident submarines.

Defence Exports

The Defence Export Services Organisation (DESO) has a budget of £73 million to promote the export of British defence equipment. UK defence exports amount to about £5 billion a year and represent about 20 per cent of the world's export market, making us the second largest exporter.

Because of the effect on our own forces' procurement costs, the DESO reports to the MoD's Chief of Defence Procurement. The government estimates that defence exports reduced the UKs own defence expenditure by about £300 million, due to the sharing of programme overheads and by allowing longer production runs. Most of these sales are financially underpinned by the ECGD, see Chapter 6.

The Royal Air Force

RAF, 1996-97

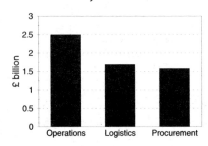

1995-96 manpower of 68,000 is being reduced by 8,000, by April 1997. The Volunteer Reserve and the Royal Auxiliary Air Force provide an extra 11,000 personnel.

Major RAF Equipment[1]

Type	Number	Role
Fixed wing aircraft:		
Tornado GR1s	142	Strike (78), reconnaissance (26), training (38)
Tornado F3s	107	Air defence (86), training (21)
Harriers	68	Offensive (51), training (17)
Jaguars	54	Offensive (30), Reconnaissance(14), training (10)
Hawks	27	target towing (14), aerobatic(11), training (2)
Canberras	9	Reconnaissance
Nimrods	28	Patrol (23), reconnaissance (2), training (3)
E-3D Sentry	7	Airborne Early Warning (AEW)
VC10s	14	Transport, refuelling
Tristars	9	Refuelling
Hercules	55	Transport (49), training (6)
BAe 125 & 126	11	Transport
Helicopters:		
Chinook	34	Troop transport (27), training (7)
Sea King	23	Search and Rescue (20), training (3)
Wessex	42	Troop transport (38), training (4)
Puma	37	Troop transport (32), training (5)

1 As at 1 April 1996

The attrition rate can be alarmingly high: in the first two months of 1996 six aircraft were lost - three Tornados, a Jaguar, a Harrier and a Hawk - with the Navy also losing two Sea Harriers.

The three major procurement projects at present are:

- the joint development of the Eurofighter, of which we have ordered 232 to be delivered from the year 2001. The total cost of the project, shared with other European countries, is expected to be around £15 billion;

- 22 Westland EH101 and 14 Chinooks to replace our Wessex support helicopters and to cover anticipated attrition losses of existing Chinooks; and

- 25 C-130J Hercules transports, to replace half the current fleet.

The helicopter orders, placed in March 1995, highlighted the dilemma often faced in large defence contracts. The RAF wanted Boeing Chinooks but, in the interests of maintaining jobs at Westland and their suppliers, an extra £300 million was spent and the order split.

Logistic support for the RAF includes the upgrading of all Tornado GR1s to GR1B specification. And the Tornado F-3s which will start to be replaced by the Eurofighter in 2001 are, in the meantime, getting a £125 million upgrade, to allow them to carry new medium- and short-range air-to-air missiles. The upgraded aircraft will come into service in 1998.

Security and Intelligence Agencies

These include the Government Communications Headquarters (GCHQ) at Cheltenham, the Secret Intelligence Service (SIS, or MI6), and the Security Service (MI5). The total manpower of the agencies is believed to be roughly 5,000.

Spending details are not available, of course, but the government has recently clarified their overall expenditure by bringing it into a single Cabinet Office Vote. Previously it had been hidden within the Ministry of Defence and Foreign Office budgets.

Although it is difficult to obtain detailed information about their activities it has become clear that MI6 are as active as ever in the former Soviet Union. But now, rather than countering a perceived direct threat, one task is to discover to whom the great military-industrial complex is selling the arms that it produces.

MI5 have been largely employed on anti-terrorist work in Northern Ireland, but the lull created by the 1995 ceasefire allowed some personnel to be hired by the police, particularly for anti-drugs work.

Defence Agencies

Since 1990 there has been a programme to review all the defence support functions to see whether they can be privatised or helped to deliver services internally on a more "business-like" basis. As a result 29 Next Steps agencies have been set-up within the MoD and several have moved on to Trading Fund status. One of these, the Defence Evaluation and Research Agency (DERA), formed from the Defence Research Agency and several smaller research establishments, has a turnover of more than £1 billion and is the government's largest trading fund. It expects to make savings of some £270 million over the next five years through reducing its overheads and gaining external customers.

The Meteorological Office has also recently become a trading fund and now charges the MoD £55 million a year for its services. Its total turnover, including work for other government departments and for the private sector, is some £150 million.

Other Procurement

In addition to the procurement costs in the bar charts above, some procurement affects more than a single armed service:

Nuclear weapons	£309 million
Conventional weapons & electronic systems	£619 million
Communications & information systems	£397 million
Other	£796 million

The first of these covers the costs of the Atomic Weapons Establishments at

Aldermaston and Burghfield. The communications systems include the manufacture and placing into orbit of three SKYNET 4, Stage 2, communications satellites to replace the current Stage 1 constellation. The main items in "Other" are the running costs of the Procurement Executive and support to the Export Credit Guarantee Department in connection with credit arrangements for certain defence exports, but the separate figures are not available.

Policy and Management

The £670 million budget of the 2nd Permanent Under Secretary of State for Defence (2nd PUS) includes all central administrative expenditure of the MoD, and rent and maintenance costs of the civil element of the Defence estate.

Management and support services closer to operations come under the budget of the Vice Chief of Defence Staff, who is responsible for the rest of the Defence estate including overseas bases and married quarters. His £1,550 million also includes the cost of arms control monitoring, and subscriptions of £79 million and £63 million respectively to NATO's military budget and infrastructure project.

The 2nd PUS and the Vice Chief of Defence Staff together plan and monitor all defence spending.

Pension Payments

As is the case for all other public sector employees, there is no pension fund for members of the armed forces. Superannuation payments made by them or on their behalf, which are included above with all other personnel costs, are used to directly pay the pensions of retired servicemen and women. But with the numbers in the forces substantially lower than a few years ago, the money coming in is well short of what is needed to meet current pension obligations. In 1990-91 the gap was only £300 million, but the government now has to make up a difference of £1,085 million.

Further Information

Ministry of Defence: The Government's Expenditure Plans 1996-97 to 1998-99. Cm 3202, HMSO.

Supply Estimates 1996-97. HC 261, HMSO.

Statement on the Defence Estimates, 1996. Cm 3223, HMSO.

Statement on the Defence Estimates 1995: Stable Forces in a Strong Britain. Cm 2800, HMSO.

Ministry of Defence Annual Report, 1995. Cm 2801, HMSO.

As our economic position in the world declines we seek to maintain political influence to support our national interests, through bilateral diplomacy, through our membership of the United Nations, NATO and the European Union and - less directly - through aid. These activities are handled by the two arms of the Foreign and Commonwealth Office (FCO): the Overseas Development Administration (ODA) and the Diplomatic Wing.

International Relations
1996-97: £3,408 million

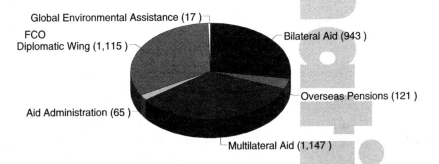

Global Environmental Assistance (17)
FCO Diplomatic Wing (1,115)
Bilateral Aid (943)
Overseas Pensions (121)
Aid Administration (65)
Multilateral Aid (1,147)

Bilateral aid involves only ourselves and the receiving countries, and so is the money that the ODA has direct control over, both in terms of the total amount and how it is spent. *Multilateral* aid is so-named because it comprises our contributions to pooled resources of many countries, held and allocated by organisations like the European Community, the International Monetary Fund and UN agencies.

On the chart, we assume that the aid budget's Contingency Reserve is used, and spent on bilateral aid.

Bilateral Aid

Our bilateral aid goes to about 170 countries, but the great majority receive only quite small sums. The top ten recipients in 1994-95 accounted for 38 per cent the total budget:

Major Recipients of Bilateral Aid, 1994-95

	£ million	
India	83	
Bangladesh	46	
Former Yugoslavia	45	
Rwanda	45	(emergency aid)
Zambia	39	
Uganda	36	
Russia	33	
China	28	
Kenya	28	
Pakistan	28	

Most of the money goes to the poorest developing countries, including one third to Africa, but about £80 million a year now goes to countries of the former Soviet Union and Eastern bloc.

Aid is provided in many forms. In 1994-95 it was allocated as follows:

Bilateral Aid
1994-95: £1,146 million

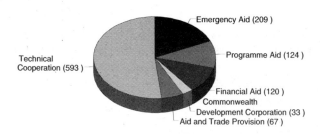

Emergency Aid (209)
Programme Aid (124)
Technical Cooperation (593)
Financial Aid (120)
Commonwealth Development Corporation (33)
Aid and Trade Provision (67)

A full breakdown of plans for 1996-97 is not available, but gross spending (which includes the use of £88 million of receipts) will be about £115 million lower.

The UN Target for Aid

Uniquely amongst the government's main expenditure programmes, the aid budget has an internationally agreed spending target. Britain is notionally committed to meeting the UN's target of 0.7 per cent of GNP, although we have never set a date for reaching it. Instead, the budget is less than half of this and falling:

Overseas Aid

1996-97 sees the second successive year in which the level of aid has declined even in cash terms.

Scandinavian countries are much more generous with their giving - Norway, Denmark and Sweden each give more than 1 per cent of GNP. Of the major economies of Europe, France does best with 0.6 per cent. Perhaps we are more inclined than others to follow the poor example of the United States which gives only 0.2 per cent.

Emergency Aid

In many people's minds aid is associated with the relief of famine and disaster, but in fact only about 10 per cent of the total aid budget is used in this way. In 1994-95, it was spent as follows:

Disaster relief	£143m
Food Aid	£36m
Refugee relief	£26m
Other	£3m

By its nature, of course, spending on emergency aid cannot be predicted. So only £65 million is budgeted in total for 1996-97, but this is can be supplemented from a contingency reserve of £60 million within the aid budget, and through reallocations of other funds, if the need arises.

Programme Aid
This represents financial support to countries that are undertaking economic reform under Structural Adjustment Programmes, to help pay for essential imports and public services.

Financial Aid
This is the money provided for specific projects that recipients can spend themselves, as they think best. But most project support is still provided as UK goods and services paid for by the ODA and supplied through Technical Cooperation, see below.

The Commonwealth Development Corporation
The CDC provides loans, equity funds and management services to local business enterprises and has about £1500 million already invested in 54 countries. So its £16 million from the 1996-97 aid budget belies the scale of its activity: the income from its investments, at a target 8 per cent return, and other self-generated income, bring to about £300 million the funds it has available for further loans.

The Aid and Trade Provision
This was started by the Labour government in 1978 to help fund development projects that are of industrial and commercial significance to the UK. Although the schemes supported are supposed to meet the same appraisal criteria as other aid projects, the notorious Pergau Dam was not the only ATP project that seems to have had much more to do with supporting British business than with development. The National Audit Office and internal ODA evaluations have criticised several others, especially other large-scale energy schemes.

But while the large British contractors that profit from the ATP claim the benefits are worth about three times the value of the aid, a House of Commons Foreign Affairs Committee's report in 1994 was concerned at "the apparent lack of substantial evidence that the ATP does produce identifiable benefits to the UK".

Technical Cooperation
This covers a wide range of activities connected with the transfer of knowledge and know-how to recipient countries.

In 1994-95 the spending was as follows:

Technical Cooperation
1994-95: £593 million

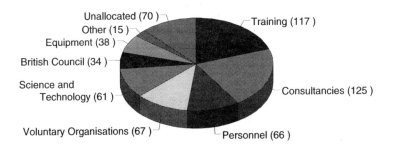

Unallocated (70) — Training (117)
Other (15)
Equipment (38)
British Council (34)
Science and Technology (61) — Consultancies (125)
Voluntary Organisations (67) — Personnel (66)

The consultants are mainly UK civil engineers and agriculturalists. Overseas visits by other experts, such as academics or civil servants, are often funded by the British Council who thus receive money from the aid budget as well as from the Diplomatic Wing, see below.

More than half the expenditure through voluntary organisations is on the Joint Funding Scheme, involving nearly 2,000 overseas projects coordinated by British non-government organisations. Most of the rest of the money - £22 million in 1994-95 - supports the volunteer programme of Voluntary Service Overseas (VSO).

Much of the science and technology funding is spent with the Natural Resources Institute (NRI) executive agency. The NRI also does an increasing amount of work for non-ODA clients.

Overseas Pensions

Civil servants of former colonies were appointed on behalf of the Foreign Secretary and were employees of the Crown, so Britain is responsible for the pre-independence element of their pensions. This spending is included in the aid programme. For reasons that are not clear, the cost of these pensions is expected to increase by £20 million in 1997-98, before falling back to around the current level the following year.

Multilateral Aid

Since 1990-91 multilateral aid has been growing at the expense of the bilateral programmes, because of increasing contributions to the EC aid programme.

Some of this we give voluntarily but most of it is levied by various international organisations to which Britain belongs. These are mainly specific development organisations, but the EC also likes to have an aid programme it can call its own. Funding of these agencies is much easier to predict than the bilateral programme, so 1996-97 data are available:

Multilateral Aid
1996-97: £1,147 million

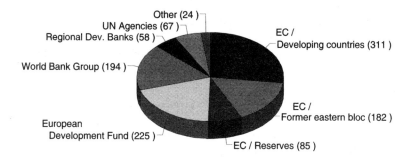

Other (24)
UN Agencies (67)
Regional Dev. Banks (58)
World Bank Group (194)
EC / Developing countries (311)
EC / Former eastern bloc (182)
EC / Reserves (85)
European Development Fund (225)

Half of the money goes into the EC aid budget, including a substantial amount for Central and Eastern Europe and Central Asia. Some of this is to help prepare Central European countries for membership of the EU.

The European Development Fund, also operated by the EC, finances the aid component of the Fourth Lomé Convention on aid and trade with the African, Caribbean and Pacific countries.

£167 million of the money for the World Bank group goes to the International Development Association, which supports poverty reduction and sustainable development programmes in low-income countries. A further £20 million contributes to an Interest Subsidy Account of the IMF's Enhanced Structural Adjustment Facility, to help reduce the burden of loan charges of developing countries borrowing from the IMF.

Our largest contribution to regional development banks is to the European Bank for Reconstruction and Development, giving £40 million in 1994-95. The EBRD lends money at near-market rates to businesses in central and eastern Europe and Central Asia, to help develop their private sectors and assist their transition towards market-oriented economies.

The £67 million to UN agencies is distributed as follows:

Contributions to UN Development Agencies, 1996-97

	£ million
Development Programme (UNDP)	24
Children's Fund (UNICEF)	8
Population Fund (UNFPA)	8
Industrial Development Organisation (UNIDO)	4
High Commission for Refugees (UNHCR)	5
World Health Organisation (WHO)	6
Food and Agriculture Organisation (FAO)	12

FCO Diplomatic Wing

The main spending by the Diplomatic Wing is on the diplomatic service but there are several other important items:

FCO Diplomatic Wing
1996-97: £1,115 million

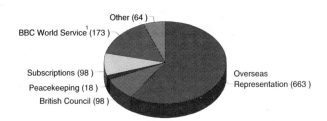

1 Includes £4 million from the MoD towards the cost of the Monitoring service.

A Fundamental Expenditure Review in 1995 identified substantial potential efficiency savings, so a 20 per cent reduction in spending, over previous plans, is expected by 1998-99.

Overseas Representation

We have diplomatic relations with 188 countries. These relations are maintained through 43 High Commissions in Commonwealth countries and 102 Embassies in other countries, together with a number of subordinate posts. The FCO also provides diplomatic representation to nine international organisations.

Most of the £663 million is spent on paying about 6,000 British and 7,500 locally engaged staff, and on other running costs. More of these resources are now applied to commercial work - mainly the promotion of UK exports - than on diplomatic activity. Other functions include entry clearance, helping British nationals abroad and providing information about Britain and her policies.

Conferences on international affairs are held at the FCO's Wilton Park centre in West Sussex to promote analysis and dialogue, and the UK's reputation for seeking mutual understanding and peaceful conflict resolution. Thirty to forty conferences are held a year, some of them on a purely commercial basis, allowing the centre to almost cover in full its £1.5 million costs.

The British Council

This is Britain's main cultural ambassador abroad but also promotes co-operation in science, technology and education. It runs about 200 libraries and information centres worldwide and about 80 English language teaching centres. As with our diplomatic representation, it has recently expanded into Central and Eastern Europe. Its total funding of £130 million from the Diplomatic Wing and the aid budget comprises only half of its income; most of the rest is generated by work for paying clients, especially in education and training.

Peacekeeping

The £18 million is a notional budgetary sum only: actual spending is likely to be much higher, drawing money from the government's general contingency reserve. At least £180 million has been spent in each year since 1992-93. Our recent activity in support of UN peacekeeping is discussed in Chapter 2.

The FCO pays Britain's 6.6 per cent assessed contribution to all the UN's peacekeeping operations, totalling about £150 million in 1995-96. It also fully reimburses the MoD's costs - budgeted at £110 million in 1996-97 - and submits claims for these to the UN. Because some other countries do not pay their assessed contributions the UN doesn't have enough money to reimburse in full. We are lucky if we get back half our costs.

Subscriptions to International Organisations

Membership of the UN, NATO and other smaller organisations incurs obligatory subscriptions, most of which are paid by the Diplomatic Wing.

International Subscriptions
1996-97: £98 million

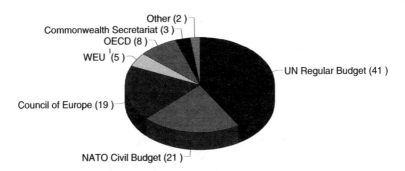

Other (2)
Commonwealth Secretariat (3)
OECD (8)
WEU (5)
Council of Europe (19)
NATO Civil Budget (21)
UN Regular Budget (41)

1 The WEU subscription includes £2 million from the MoD.

Britain is doing what it can to reduce these subscriptions, which are expected to rise to 9 per cent of the Diplomatic Wing's budget by 1998-99. This can only be done by reducing the organisations' spending, as our contributions are assessed according to the following percentages of the their budgets:

UK Share of Budget

UN Regular Budget	5.3%
NATO Civil Budget	18.9%
Council of Europe	15.6%
OECD	6.3%
Western European Union	17.0%

BBC World Service

The cost of the BBC's World Service broadcasting, to 140 million listeners worldwide in 42 languages, is financed at present entirely by the Foreign Office. But it is now being asked to find private finance for capital projects including a new transmitter in Oman. It is hoped that such schemes will absorb most of a £13 million cut in spending, compared with previous plans, over the three years to 1998-99.

As well as broadcasting, the World Service runs the BBC Monitoring operation based at Caversham, that monitors and reports on foreign radio output. This costs £18 million in 1996-97, including a contribution of £4 million from the MoD. From 1997-98, instead of receiving its funding through the World Service it will charge FCO and MoD users directly for specific services.

Global Environmental Assistance

This small budget contributes to two other international funds - in this case to support developing countries' actions to protect the environment. They are the Global Environment Facility and the Multilateral Fund of the Montreal Protocol on ozone depleting substances.

Further Information

Foreign and Commonwealth Office 1996 Departmental Report. The Government's Expenditure Plans 1996-97 to 1998-99. Cm 3203, HMSO.

British Aid Statistics (Annual). Overseas Development Administration.

British Council Annual Report and Accounts. Press and Public Relations Dept., The British Council, 10 Spring Gardens, London SW1A 2BN.

Education not only provides industry with its workers but helps mould the citizens of tomorrow's society. The money spent, especially on our schools, represents a long-term investment in both respects.

Education, 1996-97
£37.8 billion

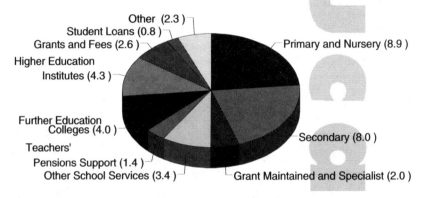

Other (2.3)
Student Loans (0.8)
Grants and Fees (2.6)
Higher Education Institutes (4.3)
Further Education Colleges (4.0)
Teachers' Pensions Support (1.4)
Other School Services (3.4)
Primary and Nursery (8.9)
Secondary (8.0)
Grant Maintained and Specialist (2.0)

"Other" includes spending on the Office for Standards in Education (OFSTED, £0.1 billion), education research (£0.1 billion) and the Youth Service (£0.3 billion).

While the expansion of higher education has taken place more rapidly than expected, and so sucked in more money than planned, there is a strong perception that schools are struggling to fund the demands of the National Curriculum and depend increasingly on parental support.

Nursery Education

Public education for some three and most four year olds is provided by state nursery schools, nursery classes of primary schools, and reception classes (which also include five year olds). 90 per cent of four year olds have a full or part-time place but there is enormous variation accross education authorities in the number and type of places available. Because some four year olds are admitted to primary school reception classes it is not possible to isolate the amount of money spent on teaching under-fives, but we estimate it to be between £600 and £800 million.

How Important is Nursery Education?

In its report *Learning to Succeed*, the National Commission on Education details the research on the effect that nursery education has on academic and social development, through to adult life. This has found that as well as increasing educational attainment it can also reduce the likelihood of unwanted early pregnancies and criminal behaviour. The research concludes that in the long-term, not only should increased spending on nurseries create happier children and better adjusted adults, it is also likely to pay for itself through savings on social spending.

In April 1996 the Department for Education and Employment (DfEE) began a one-year pilot of a new way of funding nursery education for the 645,000 four-year-olds in England and Wales. Parents are given vouchers worth £1100 which can be used to buy a part-time (five-session) place at either a state or a private nursery. At the same time local authorities have £1100 per child place withdrawn from their nursery funding, which they can recover from the DfEE by redeeming the vouchers. The authorities are free to continue to spend in excess of the value of the voucher if they need or wish; their problems are likely to arise from the new uncertainty of their base funding.

Only four local authorities agreed to take part in the pilot although the government wanted a dozen. If the scheme is extended countrywide in 1997 the total cost will be £750 million, comprising £565 million deducted from LA spending plus £185 million new money.

Primary and Secondary Education

There are about 24,000 primary and 5,000 secondary state schools, and child places in each cost around £1,800 and £2,300 a year respectively, excluding capital spending. 90 per cent of this pays teachers and support staff and just 4 per cent goes on books and equipment.

The 1980s saw a nearly 50 per cent increase in real spending per child but this has levelled off over the last few years, and in secondary schools has fallen along with the teacher:pupil ratio.

While all state schools in Northern Ireland are funded directly by central government, in Britain until recently they were nearly all controlled by the local education authority (LEA) - either the County or the Metropolitan District. But over the last few years the Local Management of Schools initiative has transferred control over most school-related spending to the schools themselves. So LEAs now hand over on average 90 per cent of their Potential Schools Budget to the schools, to spend as they see fit. This freedom to spend according to their own priorities has been generally welcomed.

The government is also encouraging more schools to become totally self-governing, or Grant Maintained (GM), breaking away entirely from the LEAs. It is doing this by making additional capital grants available to them, worth about £140 million in 1996-97. So far, about 1200 have opted for GM status

Work Experience

Since 1983 grants have been made to Local Education Authorities - and directly to some grant maintained schools - to help to develop schools' curricula in key subjects and to improve work experience opportunities. This Technical and Vocational Education Initiative (TVEI) is aimed at 14 to 18 year olds, helping to equip them with skills in science, technology and modern languages.

The government wants all young people to have the chance of a placement but its direct TVEI funding is now running down, with only £20 million for 1996-97, but still with over a million young people benefiting this year. It is hoped that the approach will in future continue through a TEC-funded work experience programme. In 1996-97 this is providing placements for about 450,000 young people at a cost of £7 million.

Work Experience

'At least we know you're not taking performance-enhancing drugs'

and are receiving their finance from the government's Funding Agency for Schools (FAS). The total cost of the GM schools is £1,715 million in 1996-97, and the cost of FAS administration is £13 million.

In general it seems that it is schools in more favoured areas that decide to become grant-maintained, as GM schools' truancy rates are far lower than the national average. This possibly contributes to their better examination results - 45 per cent of 15 year olds in GM comprehensives obtaining five or more GCSE grades of C or higher, compared with 40 per cent in LEA comprehensives, in 1994-95.

On the assumption that examination standards have not changed, attainment standards appear to be rising in all secondary schools. The percentage of all children (i.e. including those in grammar schools) that achieve the above GCSE standard was 43.5 per cent in 1994-95, having increased at about 2 per cent a year since 1989-90.

Assisted Places

At the 1995 Conservative Party conference John Major announced the doubling of the government's commitment to provide full or partial payment of fees for the private education of particularly able children from families with low incomes (usually less than £15,000 p.a.). There are about 30,000 places at present but the increase must phase-in over a number of years, so funding will increase by about £20 million a year over the next six years. The current level, £118 million, is included in the pie chart with other secondary school spending.

Assisted Places

Specialist Schools

The government's drive to create diversity in schools began with the creation of City Technology Colleges (CTCs), independent secondary schools set up jointly with business sponsors. The sponsors contributed nearly £40 million capital, but such business involvement was less forthcoming than the government had hoped, so only 15 were created. They are receiving funding of £55 million in 1996-97.

CTCs have been followed by a less ambitious approach to private sector partnership. Existing secondary schools can apply to become Technology or Language Colleges if they can raise about £100,000 in business sponsorship to develop their facilities. 38 schools - only about one quarter of the applicants - were accepted in 1996, determined by the funds for the programme set aside by government. This brought the total to 152 Technology and 30 Language Colleges.

The government matches the £100,000 the colleges have raised for capital improvements and then provides an additional £100 per pupil per year. The government is providing £23 million in funding for the colleges in 1996-97.

Office for Standards in Education (OFSTED)

This was set up in 1993 under Her Majesty's Chief Inspector of Schools, to encourage the improvement of school education. It recruits, trains and registers inspectors, and awards contracts to inspection teams for individual school inspections.

Schools are inspected every four years, with each inspection lasting 3-5 days and costing about £10,000 for an average primary school or £30,000 for a secondary school. Plans to also inspect nurseries add £5 million to 1996-97 costs. Concerns have been expressed that the cold-blooded inspection and reporting process is not as helpful as a more supportive approach.

Total spending this year is £93 million on inspections and another £30 million on administration, covering OFSTED's staff of 500. The work of the equivalent Office of Her Majesty's Chief Inspector of Schools in Wales costs £10 million a year.

Other School Services

About £1 billion is spent on the 1900 special schools for the 125,000 children with special educational needs. Also included in this segment of the pie chart is in-service training, under the Grants for Educational Support and

Training (GEST) programme, costing £300 million. About half of this is aimed at helping schools to improve on weak areas identified by OFSTED inspections.

The other main services are transport to school (£400 million) and school meals (£500 million). The Schools' Curriculum and Assessment Authority, responsible for the National Curriculum and for reviewing school examination and assessment systems, costs £32 million.

Teachers Pensions

The teachers' superannuation scheme, making £3.2 billion in pension payments in 1996-97, is run by the Teachers' Pensions Agency, within the DfEE. The scheme is under increasing strain from the large numbers of teachers retiring early through ill-health - at over 6,000 a year, twice the number ten years ago. The 14 per cent of salary being paid (6 per cent by the teacher and 8.05 per cent by the employer, usually the LEA) only provides £1.8 billion, so the government has to add a further £1.4 billion.

The Agency has a staff of 400 and administrative costs of £14 million. The government has invited private sector companies to tender for a contract to take over administration of the scheme.

The Youth Service

Local authorities spend about £300 million on the Youth Service, that aims to help 14 to 21 year olds develop as mature and responsible members of the community. They provide space for voluntary youth groups both in purpose-built Youth and Community Centres and by making schools facilities available, and they help in the training of volunteer youth workers.

Until 1996, central government supported the National Youth Agency that helps local authorities and the voluntary sector to improve the quality, range and effectiveness of youth work. Now, instead of providing it with a grant of £1.3 million, central government gives local authorities £0.7 million through additional Revenue Support Grant, to fund the Agency. A further £0.4 million (the same level as previously) is provided for the youth work development grants that the Agency administers.

The Department also provides £3 million a year to 63 National Voluntary Youth Organisations, for undertaking approved work with socially deprived teenagers in personal and social education, and £2.2 million in training grants and support for drugs awareness training of youth workers.

Further Education

In 1993, further education and sixth-form colleges (for 16-18 year olds) were removed from Local Authority control and became autonomous. There are now about 500 colleges, financed through three national Further Education Funding Councils (FEFCs) in England, Scotland and Wales. In Northern Ireland, further education remains the responsibility of the Department of Education for Northern Ireland.

Students study for GCSEs, GCE 'A'-Levels, skills-based National Vocational Qualifications (NVQs) and for General National Vocational Qualifications (GNVQs), which combine the vocational training of NVQs with some academic content.

80 per cent of 16 year olds now opt for further education and 68 per cent of 17 year olds, but the government is trying to improve on this, mainly by increasing the range of GNVQs available. The increasing numbers are accompanied by lower spending per full-time student: current spending of £2,680 is down about 17 per cent in real terms on 1990.

After major investment when the colleges first became self-governing, capital grants to the FEFCs are now falling, with those in England receiving £110 million in 1996-97.

Higher Education

This covers all education at universities (including the former polytechnics), independent teacher training colleges in England and Wales, Scottish central institutions and other institutions leading to qualifications higher than GCE A-level. Entrance has grown rapidly in recent years, nearly doubling since 1989 to include 30 per cent of those leaving school or further education. The number of students is now over one million full-time equivalents and is intended to stabilise, but with an increase in the proportion of mature students as the number of school leavers falls for demographic reasons.

In 1993 the Universities Funding Council and the Polytechnics and Colleges Funding Council (PCFC) were replaced by three national Higher Education Funding Councils (HEFCs), mirroring the new structure for the funding of further education. The £3.4 billion 1996-97 grants, by the HEFC for England to its 170 universities and colleges, represent a cut of 5 per cent on the previous year. Money for capital spending, at £243 million, is down 31 per cent.

Teacher Training

In 1994 the Teacher Training Agency (TTA) was set up in England to bring together all responsibilities relating to the training of teachers and the improvement of standards within the profession. In Wales the responsibility for teacher training remains with the higher education colleges and the University of Wales.

In 1995, 16,000 people obtained post-graduate certificates in education (PGCEs) and 10,400 gained first degrees with Qualified Teacher Status, but there is a growing shortage of trained teachers. The TTA's budget has been sharply increased from £130 million, in 1995-96, to £200 million, to help it meet ambitious targets for expansion. These, set by the DfEE, are to increase its intake of future secondary teachers by 50 per cent by the year 2001, and primary teachers by 34 per cent.

Moreover, the course fees paid by local education authorities (reimbursed by central government), which had been increasing to form a much higher proportion of funding than in the past, have been frozen at 1995-96 levels. These rates vary from £750 per student for classroom-based courses to £2,800 for clinical elements of medical courses. The total cost of student fees will be about £1.1 billion in 1996-97.

The shift towards payment according to student numbers has encouraged universities to rapidly increase their intakes and so reduce their real unit cost per student - by about 25 per cent since 1989. But the growth has been greater than the government wanted, hence the cuts, and many feel that the quality of the system is suffering in the rush to squeeze more in.

To try to maintain their income, universities are starting to look to the students themselves. Vice-Chancellors have threatened a £300 a head levy on new students in 1997 while many anticipate a move towards a tax on graduates, to replace student grants and to augment their course fees. Sir Ron Dearing, chairman of the PCFC during the years of most rapid growth, has been asked to look at the options and report in mid-1997.

Student Grants and Loans

The government has been progressively shifting the balance from grants towards loans, and for the 1996-97 academic year the rates are about equal. But while the government will pay about £1.1 billion in grants, only about £845 million is expected to be borrowed, because many students prefer not to take on such debt.

The cost of loans is offset of course by repayments but, with the scheme at a relatively early stage, these are still small - £80 million is expected this year. Past students have to make repayments once their income reaches 85 per cent of national average earnings.

The loans are administered by the Student Loans Company, set up by the government. As well as the controversy surrounding the principle of loans rather than grants, the company has come under attack for delays in the payment of loans and for alleged impropriety. This led to the head of the company being sacked in March 1995.

Further Information

The Department for Education and Employment, and Office for Standards in Education, Departmental Report 1996. Cm 3210, HMSO.

Learning to Succeed. Report of the National Commission on Education, 1993. Heinemann.

Education Statistics for the UK (Annual), HMSO.

Education Statistics, Estimates (Annual), CIPFA Statistical Information Service. (Gives detailed spending by individual LEAs.)

Local Authority Performance Indicators, March 1996, Audit Commission, HMSO.

At the interface of the worlds of education, industry, urban policy and social security lies a considerable amount of activity aimed at assisting and encouraging people into productive employment.

There are a number of government agencies involved. The Department for Education and Employment (DfEE) and the Employment Service (ES) are the largest, but similar functions to those of the DfEE are carried out by Scottish Enterprise, Highlands and Islands Enterprise, the Welsh Office's Industry and Training Department and Northern Ireland's Training and Employment Agency.

Smaller agencies include the Arbitration, Conciliation and Advisory Service (ACAS) and the Health and Safety Executive (HSE), and there is some local authority involvement.

Employment and Training
1996-97: £4,000 million

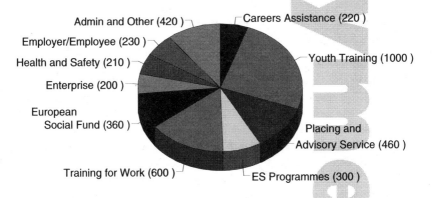

Admin and Other (420)
Employer/Employee (230)
Health and Safety (210)
Enterprise (200)
European Social Fund (360)
Training for Work (600)
Careers Assistance (220)
Youth Training (1000)
Placing and Advisory Service (460)
ES Programmes (300)

The number of agencies involved, the blurred boundaries with other departments and the uneven coverage of employment and training in the DfEE's 1996 Departmental Report make this a difficult area to tie down firmly, hence the rounded figures.

Young people are now usually introduced to the world of work through work experience placements in their final year at school, discussed in the previous chapter. Here we continue a roughly chronological treatment of the services provided to help people find suitable work.

Careers Assistance

In 1994, central government took from LEAs the responsibility for vocational guidance in England. Initially it continued to pay LEAs to provide it, from the then Employment Department budget rather than through the Revenue Support Grant, but this provision has now been almost entirely replaced by contracting out to private service providers. These operate over 100 Careers Services, counselling young people on GCSE options and post-16 and post-18 choices.

Beyond school, the government has made arrangements with several banks to provide Career Development Loans to pay for individuals' training. The government pays the interest on the loans and acts as guarantor. This scheme, together with a similar but smaller one for small firms' employees, costs £15 million a year.

Youth Training

After leaving school, 16 and 17 year olds are guaranteed suitable work-based training leading to National Vocational Qualifications (NVQs) if they want it. This is either through Youth Training or Modern Apprenticeships, coordinated and administered by the TECs. Youth Training is for one to two years either with an employer or industrial training provider, and seeks to achieve a skill standard of NVQ level 2. Modern Apprenticeships are entirely work-based, usually last three years and work to NVQ level 3 or above. About 200,000 people start one or other course of training each year.

Allowances of £29.50 per week are paid to 16 year olds and £35 to older people. The employer often adds to this. To encourage take-up, school leavers are given Youth Credits (Skillseekers in Scotland) which can be used to obtain the appropriate approved training.

Tailoring Further Education

There is a limit to the help that can be given to individuals if they cannot find training in the skills that are locally required. So the DfEE is providing a Competitiveness Fund of £20 million a year for investment by colleges of further education to help them provide new courses agreed by the TEC, regional Government Office and the Further Education Funding Council. A similar Development Fund provides another £10 million.

The government is also encouraging employers to invest more in training. Its main initiative is its *Employer Investment in People* programme through which TECs sell the business benefits of good training and try to obtain formal commitments from companies to work to develop and improve their training systems, and to strive towards the *Investors in People* national standard for good training practice. The programme costs about £60 million a year and some 21,000 organisations in England have committed themselves to reaching the standard.

The Placing and Advisory Service

This is the main service operated by the Employment Service, through its 1,100 Jobcentres throughout Great Britain. These advertise vacancies notified to them and provide advice to unemployed clients on the best way of getting back to work. They find jobs for about two million people a year. The ES staff are also responsible, from October 1996, for drawing up Job Seeker's Agreements with people claiming the Job Seeker's Allowance. Benefits Agency staff in the Jobcentres administer the Allowance itself.

A new computer system, the Labour Market System (LMS) costing £70 million, is being developed to support the Jobseeker's Agreement and other job placement work.

Employment Service Programmes

As well as directing people to the appropriate training schemes above, there are also numerous programmes run by the ES itself. The main ones, with their 1996-97 costs and the numbers of people using the programmes, are as follows:

Programme	£ million	Opportunities
Grant to Remploy Ltd	94	9,500
Supported Employment	60	12,000
Jobclub	36	183,000
PACT	28	226,000
1-2-1	16	240,000
Jobplan Workshops	16	150,000
Access to Work	14	9,500
Restart Courses	9	76,500
Workwise	7	30,000

Remploy is a government-sponsored company that finds suitable employment for people whose severe disabilities prevent them earning a normal salary. Remploy make up the difference between this and what the host employer can afford to pay them. The other **supported employment** spending is similar, but the sponsors are voluntary bodies and local authorities.

Disabled people who could gain work with other employers, given appropriate personal or technical support, can have this provided through **Access to Work**.

People previously receiving Invalidity or Sickness Benefit who do not qualify for the more stringent Incapacity Benefit are regarded as being fit to take some kind of work, but may not have worked for a long time. **Placing, Assessment and Counselling Teams** - PACTs - have been formed to help provide the support required to overcome the particular difficulties experienced by this group in finding work.

Project Work

This is a scheme being piloted in Hull and Maidstone for people unemployed for two years or more. The first 13 weeks involve advice and training and/or work trials, following which the 6,000 or so participants are expected to find jobs with voluntary organisations, typically involving gardening, decorating or construction. Failure to participate will result in the withdrawal of state benefits for one or several weeks. The scheme is similar to the American Workfare system except that the work done is not for the public sector.

Project Work

Jobclubs provide people unemployed for over six months with two weeks' teaching and guidance in job-hunting skills and methods, followed by the free use of facilities (telephone, stationery etc.) to help them find work.

The week-long **Jobplan Workshops,** for people over 24 who have been unemployed for over a year, are designed to identify skills, improve confidence and generate motivation towards job-seeking and/or training. **Restart courses** are similar but last two weeks and are for those still unemployed after two years. They also directly include the making of job applications.

1-2-1, also for the long-term unemployed but unlimited in age, is a series of interviews with ES advisers to discuss the individual's next moves with respect to obtaining employment or appropriate training.

Workwise courses (Worklink in Scotland) are specifically for young adults, 18-24, who have not worked for a year or more and usually follow on from the 1-2-1 programme, if this has not been successful in helping the individual to find a job. They combine morning training workshops with afternoon jobsearch activity, last four weeks and are run by external providers.

Training for Work

This is the principal form of help for people out of work for more than six months. After assessment, a tailored programme is put together to help the individual to acquire the skills, and possibly qualifications, to help them get a job. The Employment Service does not coordinate this programme, which is contracted out by central government to the LECs and TECs, see below, but 80 per cent of starts arise from ES referrals. People who have been out of work for more than a year are given priority access, and in coalfield areas all unemployed are eligible.

Through changing from payment per trainee to payment by results, the government now expects at least 45 per cent of leavers to have a job six months after their training, rather than fewer than 40 per cent previously. Across Britain, about 250,000 people a year start a Training for Work programme.

TECs

Most of the DfEE's employment spending is on programmes run by the 75 Training and Enterprise Councils (TECs) in England. These are independent employer-led companies. The Welsh Office similarly provides most of its £150 million employment and training budget to Wales' seven TECs. The 22 similar Local Enterprise Companies (LECs) in Scotland are funded by Scottish Enterprise and Highlands and Islands Enterprise.

As well as having responsibility for Youth Training, Modern Apprenticeships, Training for Work and the Technical and Vocational Education Initiative (TVEI), TECs also provide services to the Department of Trade and Industry and the Department of the Environment.

The TECs themselves subcontract work to local training providers. The idea of having such a decentralised system, coordinated by business leaders, is to try to make the training appropriate to the local job market.

Originally funded according to the number of people simply put onto courses, a proportion of their payment is now linked to successful outcomes to encourage efforts to reduce the drop-out rate and improve the quality of training. The government now claims that TECs' costs are only around £4,750 for every successful candidate, compared with the average of £7,600 for further education colleges, which receive only ten per cent of their funding according to students' performance. The colleges argue that the comparison does not take account of the higher capital requirements of many of the courses they offer.

As well as ear-marked funding, the government provides £20 million a year of performance-related bonuses, for TECs to spend on locally important training needs that they have identified.

European Social Fund

The European Social Fund aims at improving job opportunities throughout the EU, particularly for the long-term unemployed and other disadvantaged groups, and so co-finances vocational training and employment assistance programmes. All ESF grants relating to England are approved, administered and monitored by the DfEE on behalf of the European Commission.

Of the roughly £680 million of ESF receipts used in 1996-97, around £360 million supports non-government vocational guidance, training and job creation projects. The rest supports schemes delivered by TECs and the Employment Service, and is included in the costs of these in the pie chart.

The grants to the private sector should help about 800,000 people but there have been long administrative delays in getting funds to the projects that have been awarded them, so a number have collapsed. The Department and the Commission blame each other.

In addition to the ESF, there is a small amount of money from the European Regional Development Fund for the development of approved training courses in targeted disadvantaged areas.

Promoting Enterprise

This covers a range of activities to make the provision and the seeking of employment easier. It is largely focused on the needs of small businesses and includes efforts to evaluate and minimise the burdens placed on them by official regulations.

The TEC-run Out of School Care scheme, costing £10 million, provides advice and funds to help set up new childcare projects to help parents of young children to be free to work. About 6,000 new places will be created through the help of the scheme this year.

Under the Youth Enterprise Initiative, £2 million a year is given to the Prince's Youth Business Trust to provide advice and financial help to disadvantaged, disabled or long-term unemployed young people needing capital to start up a new business. The Trust is also supported by private donations, leading to a total expenditure of £4.3 million in 1996-97. The Welsh TECs' Business Start-Up scheme provides similar help to people setting-up in business, and costs £22 million.

Firms with fewer than 50 employees can send one of them on a Skills for Small Businesses training course provided by a TEC, to develop their assessment and training skills and so allow them in turn to develop their companies' own training programmes. The initiative will be complete when 24,000 'key employees' have been thus trained, by 1998-99. Spending in 1996-97 is £27 million.

Enterprise in rural areas has an additional dimension, in simply maintaining a viable local economy. The Rural Development Commission receives £39 million from the DoE to promote the economic and social well-being of the rural areas of England, helping to provide business accommodation (£9 million), promoting rural services (£4 million) and carrying out a number of development programmes (£8 million). Its running costs are £11 million a year. The Development Board for Rural Wales (£10 million) has a similar function while north of the border Scottish Enterprise is responsible, in addition to its main training function.

Health and Safety

Each year over 400 people are killed at work and about half a million injuries are recorded. As well as the personal tragedies these figures represent, the economic cost is enormous. 30 million working days are lost and the total cost to business and the taxpayer is over £16 billion each year.

The Health and Safety Executive has a staff of just over 4,000, most of whom are employed to carry out its annual 110,000 or so inspections of high-risk premises, e.g. mines, nuclear sites and railways. It has warned the government that its £178 million for 1996-97 - six per cent down on the previous year - will not be adequate for it to fully carry out its remit.

Local authorities' Environmental Health departments are responsible for enforcement of Health and Safety regulations in lower risk industries, spending about £35 million on inspections and related work.

Employer/Employee Relations

The Department of Trade and Industry makes redundancy payments to, and meets other entitlements of, employees whose businesses have become insolvent. These payments and their administration cost about £170 million.

Despite its relatively high profile, ACAS costs only £23 million a year. It is best known for its role as mediator in industrial disputes but has a general remit to promote the improvement of industrial relations, and works at the avoidance as well as settlement of disputes. It handles about 90,000 individual and about 1,300 collective conciliation cases a year, achieving a settlement in about 85 per cent of cases.

Industrial tribunals cost £37 million. They refer many cases to ACAS, successfully avoiding 70 per cent of them from going forward to a hearing.

Further Information

The Department for Education and Employment, and Office for Standards in Education, Departmental Report 1996. Cm 3210, HMSO.

Competitiveness - forging ahead. May 1995. Cm 2867, HMSO.

Trade and Industry. The Government's Expenditure Plans 1996-1997 to 1998-1999. DTI et al. Cm 3205, HMSO.

In a world of increasing competition, particularly from the low-wage developing economies of the east, Britain's industry must continuously reduce costs and develop new products to maintain its share of the markets. Apart from helping finance exports, the government largely lets big business look after itself while helping small, new, innovative enterprises to develop.

The government also has the liabilities of old industries to deal with, in the shape of coal and the magnox nuclear power plants.

Industry, 1996-97
£3,430 million

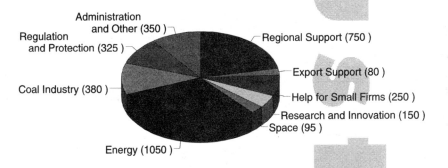

Administration and Other (350)
Regulation and Protection (325)
Coal Industry (380)
Energy (1050)
Regional Support (750)
Export Support (80)
Help for Small Firms (250)
Research and Innovation (150)
Space (95)

This chart does not include the £1.3 billion funding of pure science, which we look at later in the chapter. But formally acknowledging the place of science in securing our future prosperity, the Office of Science and Technology recently moved from the Office of Public Service to the Department of Trade and Industry (DTI).

Regional Support

The programme of Regional Selective Assistance (RSA) provides discretionary grants to attract employment-generating investment to designated Assisted Areas. In 1996-97 about £120 million is being spent in England, £55 million in Wales and £70 million in Scotland. Individual grants can be very large, such as the £48 million given to Ford to help build a new Jaguar range in the Midlands, in July 1995. It is estimated that the RSA programme generates or safeguards about 25,000 jobs each year.

In Northern Ireland's equivalent of RSA, £92 million of support is provided to industry by the province's Department for Economic Development.

The DTI, with the DoE, is responsible for securing Britain's share of EC Structural Funds, including European Regional Development Fund (ERDF) support. This must be used for capital schemes in designated disadvantaged areas, and is providing £122 million in 1996-97 for economic development of disadvantaged regions of England. £34 million is going to projects to support industry in Wales, £118 million in Scotland and £53 million for Northern Ireland. The government is trying to use ERDF funds to lever in increasing amounts of private investment, particularly with its Regional Challenge competition through which the funds for England and Wales are allocated to schemes that will provide best value for money by attracting additional capital.

Inward investment by foreign companies looking for a foot in the European market is fiercely fought for. As well as the DTI's *Invest in Britain* Bureau (£3 million), each region has its own agency to encourage and help potential investors to locate here. England's eight Regional Development Organisations receive a total of £9 million in government grants and claim to create or safeguard about 20,000 jobs a year - costing less than £500 a job. *Locate in Scotland*, run by Scottish Enterprise, has a budget of £15 million for the same purpose and the Highlands and Islands Development Board a budget of £5 million.

The Welsh Development Agency combines property development, especially factory building, with the promotion of Wales as an industrial base. Its gross spending is around £120 million but £80 million of this is funded by sales, e.g. of factories it has built. The Agency recently gained a major coup in securing a £1.7 billion investment by the South Korean conglomerate LG, for two factories to build microchips near Newport. About 6,000 jobs will be created. The grants provided by the Welsh Development Agency and the Welsh Office are understood to be worth up to £200 million. At about £30,000 a job this is more generous than most offers and reflects the strong competition from elsewhere.

The Industrial Development Board for Northern Ireland works in a similar way, with a £9 million promotion budget on top of its £28 million (net) spending on property development activities.

'I can still remember when most British cars were Japanese'

Export Support

The DTI involves itself proactively in export promotion by setting up bilateral trade missions and spending about £45 million ensuring good UK representation at international trade fairs - around three hundred a year. But it also gathers information for British business on potential export markets.

To contest any barriers to British exports reported by exporters, its Single Market Compliance Unit takes up problems within the EU with the European Commissions, while external barriers can now be referred to the World Trade Organisation, set up in 1995 and to which we pay a £1 million subscription.

Many exporters are also helped by the Export Credits Guarantee Department (ECGD), who provide credit to overseas purchasers of expensive capital items and insurance to exporters against non-payment. Its trading activities - dominated by medium to long-term export credit guarantees but also including the reinsurance of short-term export credit and the insurance of overseas investments - do not count as public expenditure. They aim to break even in the long term but are expected to make a contribution of some £250 million to government income in 1996-97.

The ECGD's two public expenditure programmes are Fixed Rate Export Finance and Tender to Contract/Forward Exchange Supplement (TC/FES). The first provides overseas buyers with fixed-rate credit to pay for their purchases, and can lose money if borrowers default but can profit if interest rates fall below the average rate at which loans were made. In 1996-97 a loss of £8 million is expected, while about £2 billion-worth of exports are being supported. TC/FES protects exporters against changes in exchange rates between tendering and the awarding of contracts, and has costs of less than £1 million. Adminstration costs of the ECGD are about £24 million a year.

Help for Small Firms

Over the last couple of years around two hundred *Business Link* one-stop shops have been set up in England where small and medium-sized businesses can get support locally from the Department. £50 million of their £123 million funding in 1996-97 is still to cover start-up costs and £51 million is for Business Enterprise services - advice and business training provided through TECs. Business Link offices themselves have expert advisors to help with areas such as design, innovation and export. Similar networks in Scotland and Wales are known as Scottish Business Shops and Business Connect.

The Small Firms Loan Guarantee Scheme underwrites bank loans to small businesses that lack the security normally required. The government is called to honour this guarantee for about 15 - 20 per cent of loans, leading to expected costs of about £45 million in 1996-97.

To promote best practice in management, the "Managing in the '90s" programme is targeted at small and medium-sized businesses and involves seminars, workshops and the production of various teaching materials. It costs nearly £20 million a year.

In Northern Ireland the Local Enterprise Development Unit has a £32 million programme to provide advice and support to small businesses, and help business start-ups.

Industrial Research and Innovation

The DTI believes that large companies should be doing more research and development but financing it themselves, and so gives support mainly to small and medium sized firms. Companies with up to 50 employees that have good ideas can win Small firms Merit Awards for Research (SMART) funding to develop them into finished products, while medium-sized firms (with up to 250 employees) can get a Support for Products Under Research (SPUR) grant covering up to 30 per cent of the development cost. 179 SMART awards were made in 1995-96 and 233 SPUR awards; planned funding for 1996-97 is £11 million and £8 million respectively.

For larger companies the government-wide LINK programme fosters collaboration with universities on strategically important technologies, from aquaculture to waste minimisation. Funding from government (£21 million) or research councils is matched by industry, with the Office of Science and Technology, see below, having lead responsibility for the programme.

British companies are also taking advantage of the EC's 5-year EUREKA initiative to fund international collaboration in high technology research and development between companies. Britain's contribution to 1996-97 funding is about £13 million.

There are a large number of small programmes aimed at improving the transfer of new knowledge and technologies from universities to industry. Two of the larger ones are the Teaching Company Scheme (TCS) and the Information Society Initiative (ISI). The TCS targets small and medium-sized companies, sponsoring about 300 recent graduates each year to work in the companies for two years. It is funded jointly by the DTI and the Engineering and Physical Sciences Research Council at a cost of £16 million. ISI is a four-year programme, launched in 1996 with a total budget of up to £35 million, to help business develop and exploit the potential of new information and communication technologies.

The Civil Aircraft Research And Demonstration (CARAD) programme coordinates UK aeronautics research, promoting national co-operation including the transfer of technologies from defence research to civil aircraft design. It spends £23 million, most of it through the Defence Research Agency, but also on industrial research.

Sponsorship of research for the construction and property industries by the DoE costs about £17 million a year, most of which is spent on work by the Building Research Establishment, on health and safety issues as well as design and construction.

Space

Britain contributes £88 million to the European Space Agency (ESA) largely to support the development of Earth observation satellites. ERS-2 was launched in 1995 and the next, ENVISAT-1, is due in 1998. Another £7 million is spent on systems for distributing the data from observation satellites and producing useful data products, but industry is being encouraged to take a larger share of such funding.

Space research without direct practical applications is funded by the Particle Physics and Astronomy Research Council, see below under Pure Science.

Energy

The Non-Fossil Fuel Levy, charged at 10 per cent on all electricity purchases, until November 1996 when it drops to 3.7 per cent, will raise up to £850 million in 1996-97. £700-720 million of this is subsidising production from old magnox nuclear reactors.

When British Energy was created and sold, to operate the former Nuclear Electric's seven advanced gas-cooled reactors and the Sizewell B pressurised water reactor power stations, Magnox Electric plc was created with responsibility for the magnox reactors. This government-owned company will later be integrated with BNFL. With no magnox reactors, British Energy receives no proceeds from the levy.

The other £130 million of the Non-Fossil Fuel Levy pays a 'green premium' to generators using renewable sources of power, stimulating commercial development by guaranteeing a higher income per kWh.

Alternative energy sources at an earlier stage of development are receiving about £45 million of research funding in 1996-97. £21 million of this is for nuclear research, mainly nuclear fusion, while renewables get £14 million, clean coal technologies £6 million, and oil and gas production £3 million.

The fusion research is carried out by the UK Atomic Energy Authority. The UKAEA also, with British Nuclear Fuels (BNFL), receives £136 million from the Decommissioning and Radioactive Waste Management Operations and Support (DRAWMOPS) programme. Another £18 million goes to UKAEA to support its property management and other operations but its £6 million profit on all these activities goes back to the government in repayment of loans.

The Coal Industry

Two years after privatisation the coal industry is still costing the government a lot of money:

Planned Public Expenditure on the Coal Industry, 1996-97

Pension payments	£141 million
Concessionary fuel entitlements	£87 million
The Coal Authority	£60 million
British Coal: Deficiency grant	£35 million
Residual payments grant	£57 million

The Coal Authority is the formal owner of Great Britain's coal reserves and so administers the licensing of all mining operations. But most of its £60 million grant meets the cost of subsidence claims and other liabilities associated with abandoned coalfields.

The grants to British Coal are to reduce or remove its historic deficit (the Deficiency Grant) and its current cash flow deficit.

Administration and Other

The gross cost of administering the DTI is £360 million, comprised of about £340 million staff costs and £20 million capital, but this is offset by various fees and recoveries to give a net cost of £315 million. The corresponding Northern Ireland department costs £26 million.

Other spending includes £33 million on research to improve the methods of measurement and analysis used as standards in industry. Two-thirds of the funding for this *National Measurement System* goes to the National Physical Laboratory, and provides over half its income.

£7 million is paid to the *British Standards Institution*, and to industrial participants, for the writing of standards for product specification and management systems, and another £7 million goes to the *Shipbuilding Intervention Fund* to help British shipyards compete for merchant shipping contracts.

The above costs are partially offset by £65 million net income from *Launch Aid*, a programme through which the government has provided large amounts of risk capital to support the development and production of new civil aircraft and components. Having helped with the development of the Airbus A330/340 airliners and Rolls-Royce's RB211 and V2500 engines, the programme is now receiving repayments amounting, in 1996-97, to £45 million and £21 million respectively for the two projects. The only Launch Aid project currently being supported is development of the Learjet 45 by Short Brothers, receiving only £1.3 million this year after getting £20 million in 1995-96.

At the same time as paying off the debts accrued in its development, the Airbus is receiving £7 million of government support to help promote overseas sales.

Regulation of the Utilities

The privatisation of the utilities has meant the creation of several small non-ministerial government departments to protect consumers and to promote competition within specific industries. OFGAS, OFTEL, OFWAT and OFFER regulate prices, profits and other activities in the gas, telecommunications, water and electricity industries respectively. Current annual spending is as follows:

OFGAS	£8 million
OFTEL	£9 million
OFWAT	£9 million
OFFER	£10 million

These costs are recovered through licence fees levied on the respective industries, which score as government income.

Regulation and Consumer / Investor Protection

The general welfare of consumers is dealt with in different ways by several bodies. The Office of Fair Trading, costing £19 million, is a general consumer watchdog, trying to promote effective competition and discourage bad trading practices. In addition, the DTI centrally spends £25 million on consumer protection, mainly in grants to the National Association of Citizens' Advice Bureaux, Citizens' Advice Scotland and Consumer Councils. But the greatest spending, of some £170 million a year, is by the County and Metropolitan Councils that are responsible for local enforcement of trading standards.

The Monopolies and Mergers Commission carries out investigations when the government refers to it particular issues relating to potential limits to competition, that could disadvantage consumers. It receives £8 million to carry out this work.

Investors are served by the Official Receivers of the Insolvency Service, who administer and investigate bankrupt companies in England and Wales. With about 1700 employees, the Service's net costs are about £60 million in 1996-97. It has recently put more emphasis on investigating criminal activity and in 1995-96 submitted 1,250 prosecution reports. In addition, 2-300 other (i.e. solvent) companies are investigated each year by DTI inspectors, under the Companies Act, where misuse of funds or other illegal practice is suspected. This, and related work, costs £10 million.

Pure Science

Total government spending on scientific research is about £6 billion, but most of this is applied research financed by the Defence, Environment and Agriculture departments, and the Higher Education Funding Council, and covered elsewhere. Research without immediate practical application is supported by a £1.3 billion budget managed by the Office of Science and Technology (OST).

The OST is headed by the government's Chief Scientific Advisor (CSA) and is responsible for developing government policy on science and technology. The prioritisation of research is now being looked at in the context of the needs of the UK economy, working from reports produced by the Technology Foresight Programme that try to identify future market opportunities and consider the science and technology necessary in order to exploit them fully.

Most of the OST's budget is delegated to the six research councils:

The Science Budget
1996-97, £1,322 million

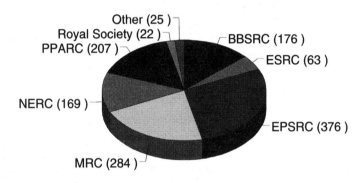

Other (25)
Royal Society (22)
PPARC (207)
BBSRC (176)
ESRC (63)
NERC (169)
EPSRC (376)
MRC (284)

BBSRC   Biotechnology and Biological Sciences Research Council
ESRC   Economic and Social Research Council
EPSRC   Engineering and Physical Sciences Research Council
MRC   Medical Research Council
NERC   Natural Environment Research Council
PPARC   Particle Physics and Astronomy Research Council

The figures shown include a total £10 million from the EU but exclude an additional £8 million of funds produced by the sale of three sites.

While most research councils' spending goes to sponsor hundreds of individual grants for university research, more than half of the PPARC's funding is passed on in subscriptions to the European Space Agency (£39 million) and European Organisation for Nuclear Research (£72 million). But it was also the PPARC that funded the development of the Cluster satellites to monitor the solar wind, which were lost when the first Ariane 5 launch failed in June 1996.

In an imaginative way of rewarding researchers for working with industry, the new Realising Our Potential Award (ROPA) scheme gives university scientists research funding for work of their own choosing if they have obtained industrial sponsorship for substantial applied research. The average size of awards is £100,000, granted from a research council's budget. Future funding depends on evaluation of the results so far, but is likely to be of the order of £50 million in 1996-97.

Further Information

Trade and Industry. The Government's Expenditure Plans 1996-1997 to 1998-1999. DTI *et al.* Cm 3205, HMSO.

Regional Industrial Policy. Cm 2910, HMSO.

The Prospects for Power in the UK. DTI and the Scottish Office. Cm 2860, HMSO.

Competitiveness: Creating the Enterprise Centre of Europe. Cm 3300, HMSO.

Forward Look of Government-funded Science, Engineering and Technology, 1995 (2 Volumes), DTI/OST. Cm 3257, HMSO.

Priorities for the Science Base: Government Response to the Second Report of the House of Lords Select Committee on Science and Technology, 1993-94. HMSO, July 1994. Cm 2636.

Most of us spend several hours a week travelling, so the speed, comfort and environmental impact of our journeys have a major impact on our own quality of life, and the quality of life of those communities we pass through. As we depend almost entirely on the government to provide the infrastructure for different modes of transport we should expect them to do so within a policy framework that considers full social costs and benefits.

Transport, 1996-97
£10.2 billion

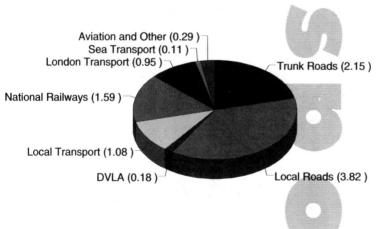

Aviation and Other (0.29)
Sea Transport (0.11)
London Transport (0.95)
National Railways (1.59)
Local Transport (1.08)
DVLA (0.18)
Trunk Roads (2.15)
Local Roads (3.82)

Trunk Roads

The Department of Transport (through the Highways Agency) and the Scottish, Welsh and Northern Ireland Offices provide and maintain the trunk road network - motorways and nearly half of the Primary Route Network. (PRN routes are those 'A' roads indicated by green signs.).

There has been much criticism in the past of the Department of Transport's apparent preoccupation with road-building. Faced with a two per cent annual increase in general traffic volume, and a virtual doubling of motorway traffic in the last ten years, the government is finally recognising that it cannot build roads fast enough to keep up (spending increased by only about 50 per cent over the decade) and is greening its transport policy. So although it still dominates transport spending, the roads budget is being reduced considerably, particularly the spending on trunk roads:

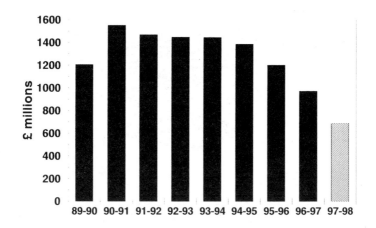

Capital Spending on Trunk Roads
England: 1996-97 prices

Most of the 1996-97 spending reductions were achieved by dropping dozens of schemes which failed to meet strict new cost-benefit and environmental criteria, but public spending on road construction is also being reduced by the use of *private* finance. The first privately financed and operated motorway will be the Birmingham North Relief Road. The Highways Agency hopes to let £1 billion worth of Design, Build, Finance and Operate contracts a year from 1996-97. The operators will be paid "shadow tolls" by the Department, according to road usage.

Capital spending accounts for only about 60 per cent of spending on trunk roads. The Highway Agency's total spending this year on England's 6,500 miles of trunk roads, including maintenance, research and other non-capital spending, is £1.6 billion.

'We've got a problem – a veal calf farm is being closed down to make way for a motorway'

Income from Road Transport

A substantial amount of tax is involved in owning and using a vehicle, so this is one area of spending where there is income from users to compare with the amount of money that is spent on them. In fact the taxes greatly outweigh the £6 billion spending on roads.

A massive £17 billion is raised from duties on fuel, but as this is now promoted by the government as a tax on pollution it might seem perverse to use it to fund more roads.

Vehicle Excise Duty raises £4.3 billion. The £140 a year on all - except vintage - cars has been criticised for taxing ownership rather than use, and the AA would like to see it scrapped. But the government likes the 'tax disc' system as a way of checking that people are also complying with MOT and insurance requirements, and it helps the DVLA to maintain its central vehicle register.

Another source of revenue, soon, will be electronic motorway tolls. The money raised will contribute to the government's general income in the same way as most other taxes, but the Department of Transport is making a strong link - at least when trying to persuade people that tolls are a good thing - between the new revenue and more spending to improve motorways.

63

Local Roads

These are those roads - including most 'A' roads - built and maintained by local authorities, which account for 96 per cent of the total road mileage. Again, about 60 per cent of the spending is capital. The DoE contributes £225 million, through the Transport Supplementary Grant, for developments relating to the 54 per cent of the PRN for which local authorities are responsible, particularly for bypass and relief road construction schemes. Mirroring reductions in trunk roads spending, the grant has fallen sharply from its peak of £430 million in 1993-94.

The DVLA and Other Transport Agencies

The Driver and Vehicle Licensing Agency is responsible for collecting Vehicle Excise Duty, and for registering and licensing drivers and vehicles. It costs £176 million in 1996-97. Driving tests are carried out by the Driving Standards Agency, which recovers its operating costs through its fees, but the government provides around £1 million to cover capital costs.

The Vehicle Inspectorate and Vehicle Certification Agency (VCA) are also more or less self-financing. The VCA is responsible for ensuring vehicle designs and production lines meet the necessary EU and domestic type-approval standards, while the Vehicle Inspectorate tries to ensure the safety of vehicles once they are on the road. As well as running the MOT testing system it carries out the testing of heavy goods vehicles itself, and enforces the laws governing their safety, e.g. relating to drivers' hours and vehicle weights.

National Railways

The operation of passenger trains is now carried out by 25 separate operating units within British Rail. The Office of Passenger and Rail Franchising (OPRAF) is letting individual franchises to private companies to operate these services, and then provides the franchisees with an agreed subsidy. Support for the non-privatised units also comes through OPRAF. The full subsidy for all units is £1.5 billion in 1996-97.

Future Rail Subsidies

Since nationalisation in 1948, British Rail has received subsidies totalling £50 billion, and the government hopes that a re-privatised system will need less support. But the Transport Select Committee of MPs doubts whether it can be reduced much below the current £1.5 billion a year, because any gains in efficiency may be outweighed by the new need to provide shareholders with dividends.

The train operators do not themselves own any rolling stock. This was sold for £1.8 billion in 1995, to three private companies who lease it back to the operators.

Railtrack, responsible for the railway network including stations and other infrastructure, was separated from British Rail in 1994 as a government company and then privatised in May 1996. The government is paying Railtrack £100 million towards the expected £650 million cost of the Thameslink 2000 project to join rail services between north and south London. New rail flyovers are to built at New Cross and Bermondsey, and the links improved between Gatwick and Stanstead.

The three regional freight businesses, Transrail, Loadhaul and Mainline were sold to Wisconsin Central Transportation in early 1996 for £225 million. The same company had already bought the mail carrier, Rail express systems. Red Star parcels and the Freightliner container service are all also to be privatised.

The Channel Tunnel Rail Link

The Eurostar service through the Channel Tunnel from Waterloo was established by European Passenger Services, a government-owned company. Another government company, Union Railways, planned the development of the 68 mile high-speed Channel Tunnel Rail Link from St Pancras to Folkestone, but in April 1996 both companies were privatised by transfer to the London & Continental consortium, which will actually build the link. The project will also involve the construction of an international station at Stratford in east London and a smaller station at Ebbsfleet in Kent.

The government has promised up to £1.4 billion (1996 prices) over the next 10 years towards the estimated £3 billion total cost, and another £100 million will come from the European Union. This subsidy can be reduced if the service starts to make large profits.

Responsibility for ensuring that all the new private companies will work together to provide a good service is vested in the Office of the Rail Regulator (ORR). With an annual budget of £8 million, ORR must ensure fairness in access to the track and in charges, ensure competition, and protect consumer interests.

Local Transport

The £1 billion is net spending - local authority car parks make a profit of about £140 million that helps to support public transport. Bus services are supported both through direct subsidy (£400 million) and through concessionary fares costing about £500 million. The government also gives rebates on fuel duty for eligible bus services, worth about 15p per bus mile and totalling some £250 million, but this is regarded as a loss of income rather than as spending.

Local rail services are subsidised by the Passenger Transport Authorities for the metropolitan districts of Merseyside, South Yorkshire, Tyne & Wear and West Midlands to the tune of £190 million. But Greater Manchester's rail services are now supported directly by OPRAF, with a £70 million subsidy, following the district's decision to withdraw support from local rail services from 1996.

In Scotland there is not the same system of funding through district councils so the Department of Transport pays, through the Scottish Office, a £70 million grant to the Strathclyde Passenger Transport Executive.

London Transport

The £950 million grant from central government is used for investment as follows:

Core business	£450 million
Jubilee Line Extension	£486 million
CrossRail	£14 million

The spending on the core business is mainly for the modernisation of the Underground system, and it is supplemented by an operating surplus of about £150 million. London Transport operations first achieved a small operating surplus in 1993-94 by increasing fares and cutting operating costs, and this surplus is expected to continue to grow.

The Jubilee Line Extension to Stratford via North Greenwich includes four new river tunnels and its total cost will be about £2 billion. It is due to open in 1998.

The CrossRail scheme, to provide a tunnel link between Paddington and Liverpool Street is being planned jointly with Railtrack and British Rail. But construction has been put off until after the completion of the other major rail projects for London.

A Private Finance Initiative deal has been used to provide and maintain over 100 new trains for the Northern Line, moving about £400 million worth of investment into the private sector.

Although still responsible for bus services throughout London, London Transport privatised the buses in 1994 and now procures the services through contracts with private operators. It pays these operators a fixed sum and itself receives all fare income. In 1994-95, the latest year for which figures are available, these were some £300 million and £240 million respectively - representing a subsidy of £60 million. In 1997 this arrangement is being replaced by net cost contracts, in which the operators receive a subsidy arrived at through a process of competitive bidding and then keep all fare receipts.

Sea Transport

The Coastguard became the Coastguard Agency in 1994 and at the same time the Marine Safety Agency (MSA) was established. While the MSA is responsible for helping to *prevent* accidents and pollution from ships, the Coastguard keeps watch for such incidents and coordinates the response to them. The Agencies cost £25 million and £53 million respectively.

Only six years ago the government was spending about £50 million a year on ports, but since then most of them have been privatised and have been repaying government loans. So public sector spending is now only around £4 million, mostly in the form of borrowing by some of the remaining Local Authority ports.

Caledonian MacBrayne, who operate ships between the Scottish islands and the mainland, receive a government subsidy of £11 million.

Aviation

The DoE is responsible for promoting safe and efficient air services in the UK. Its airport policy, aircraft pollution and accident investigation spending totals around £4 million, but its largest financial involvement is through the Civil Aviation Authority. The CAA provides air traffic control and allocates airspace, as well as regulating all civil aviation. It makes an operating profit, but has needed to supplement this with government loans to help finance investment in new air traffic control systems to increase airspace capacity. Following major investment in the early 1990s it now needs less capital, which it can meet from its operating profit, and is starting to repay the loans. The government expects to get £13 million back in 1996-97, and £23 million in 1997-98.

Local authorities still own some of the smaller airports (others have recently been privatised) and spend about £5 million a year on them, while central government provides £8 million to the Highlands and Islands Airports.

Other

The costs of the Department of Transport's Central Transport Group, that formulates transport policy and provides central services to the Department's agencies, are £84 million in 1996-97. A number of other small items contribute to the £290 million, including a contribution of £48 million to the British Rail pension fund, and £20 million on research and development.

Further Information

Department of Transport Annual Report. The Government's Expenditure Plans 1996-97 to 1998-99. Cm3206t, HMSO.

Serving Scotland's Needs. Departments of the Secretary of State for Scotland, and the Forestry Commission. The Government's Expenditure Plans 1996-97 to 1998-99. Cm 3214, HMSO.

A new British underclass is emerging, as in America, in the deprived, depersonalised and brutalised areas of our towns and cities. The violence of American city life is not yet with us but points to the direction in which we are moving. Many factors are involved, but the houses people live in and the physical and social environment outside are critical.

Reversing the trend is one of the greatest challenges to the government.

Housing and Urban
1996-97: £6.4 billion

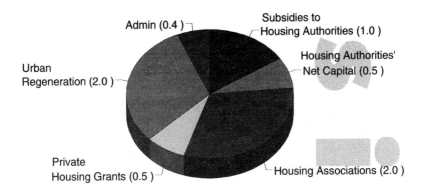

Admin (0.4)

Subsidies to Housing Authorities (1.0)

Housing Authorities' Net Capital (0.5)

Urban Regeneration (2.0)

Private Housing Grants (0.5)

Housing Associations (2.0)

The chart shows rounded estimates for most categories because recent data is not available for many items, particularly spending by local authorities.

Public Sector Housing

In England, Scotland and Wales, local authorities have responsibility for housing although in Scotland this is shared with Scottish Homes, a public corporation. Another public corporation, the Northern Ireland Housing Executive, is responsible in the Province.

The amount of public housing has been reduced over the last fifteen years both by the individual purchases by tenants of their homes and, latterly, by the Large Scale Voluntary Transfer of entire local authority housing stock to the private sector, usually Housing Associations. The numbers of homes moved from housing authority ownership by each scheme are about 1.5 million and 0.2 million respectively. The remaining stock of some 3.4 million still make up 20 per cent of homes.

These properties include a high proportion of flats and one-bedroomed dwellings inhabited by the young and the elderly, with most other houses occupied by families with unskilled or unemployed adults. As a consequence most are eligible for rent rebate.

The new Estates Renewal Challenge Fund, £33 million in 1996-97 but rising to £110 million in 1997-98, will compensate housing associations for taking over poor-condition housing estates from local authorities.

Subsidies to Housing Authorities

The housing finances of local authorities are heavily supported - and influenced - by central government. In England and Wales each authority must operate a Housing Revenue Account (HRA) which balances expenditure on repairs, maintenance, debt charges, management etc. against rent income and any central government subsidy. As well as this 'housing element' subsidy is a 'rebate element' that deals with rent rebates to tenants and their reimbursement by central government.

Each year the DoE determines the amount of HRA housing element subsidy required (if any) according to its own recommended rent increases. In practice, most authorities set rents above the government guidelines and so make a surplus on their accounts. Those still requiring subsidy receive about £720 million from central government in 1996-97 while those in surplus make a total of £1,170 million. So overall the public sector makes a profit of £450 million on council houses in England and Wales.

This profit moves from local to central government through an interaction with rent rebates. Any surplus on the housing element of the HRA must be used for rent rebate - reducing the rent rebate subsidy required from the DoE. So of the total rent rebate of £4,284 million the DoE pays only £3,114 million.

The subsidy to the Northern Ireland Housing Executive is £212 million, and to Scottish housing authorities £20 million.

Housing Authority Capital Investment

The level of capital spending on local authorities' housing stock is largely determined by the government's Housing Investment Programme (HIP). Of the DoE's £1200 million HIP only about £250 million is in the form of grants; the other £950 million is given as credit approvals - permission to borrow. Allocations are made to local authorities on the basis of need and efficiency. Authorities can then supplement their allocation by using a proportion of their receipts from council house sales. Gross capital spending on housing in 1996-97 is expected to be around £2.5 billion and is mainly on the renovation of existing stock.

Tenants of local authorities can receive money under the Cash Incentive Scheme to buy and move into their own homes. £60 million is being provided this year for the scheme, which will release 4,000 dwellings for people otherwise homeless.

Housing Associations

These non-profit-making trusts, rather than local authorities, are now the main providers of new subsidised housing. The following graph shows how they have taken over this role:

UK Social Housing Completions

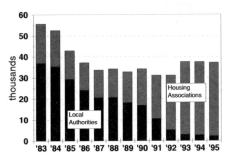

With the inclusion of stock transferred from housing authorities, they own over 600,000 homes and 55,000 hostel places. The 2,800 housing associations across Britain receive grants through the Housing Corporation (England), Scottish Homes and Housing for Wales. The 44 in Northern Ireland receive grants directly from the Department for the Environment for Northern Ireland.

The Housing Corporation's grants are made under the Approved Development Programme (ADP), funded by the DoE. The Corporation awards Housing Association Grants for individual projects through a process of competitive bidding. The ADP has fallen sharply in recent years from £1800 million in 1993-94 to just over £1 billion in 1996-97. But this government money is increasingly being supplemented by borrowing - housing associations must obtain at least 42 per cent of schemes' funding from private sources.

The government acknowledges that at least 60,000 new low cost homes for rent are needed each year but the National Federation of Housing Associations believes there is only enough money for it to build about 40,000 in 1996-97.

While most of the ADP-funded projects still provide new houses for rent, an increasing proportion goes on helping tenants to buy their own homes. This includes grants of some £80 million under the Tenants' Incentive Scheme which mirrors the Cash Incentive Scheme for local authority tenants, and helps over 6,000 people a year to buy new homes and so release their housing association tenancies to others in need.

Tenants can alternatively buy a share in their existing home and rent the remainder. Grants are paid to the associations running such schemes.

In addition to these ADP capital schemes the government provides £230 million in revenue support to the Housing Corporation, of which £130 million pays housing associations to provide 50,000 hostel places for people with special needs. The Corporation's running costs account for another £30 million.

The cost of support for Scottish housing associations through Scottish Homes is £230 million, with those in Wales receiving £95 million from Housing for Wales.

Privatisation of Housing Corporation Loans

The government's allocation to the Housing Corporation is about £500 million less in 1996-97 than it would otherwise be, because its portfolio of loans to housing associations - the Housing Corporation Loan Book - is being sold. The government treats this as a reduction in spending but we regard it in here as income, in the same way as other privatisation proceeds, and show the gross level of Housing Corporation grants to housing associations.

The same applies to the £80 million and £65 million loans portfolios being sold by Scottish Homes and Housing for Wales.

Private Housing Grants

As well as maintaining and developing their own housing stock, housing authorities provide private house renovation grants. These aim to bring homes up to the statutory fitness standard and at present are mainly mandatory. 60 per cent of the cost is reimbursed by central government, within the HIP allocations.

— Urban Regeneration —

In 1994 most English programmes that related to urban regeneration were brought into a Single Regeneration Budget (SRB), financed by the DoE and administered at the local level by the ten Government Offices for the Regions. This is intended to

Urban Regeneration
1996-97: £1,960 million

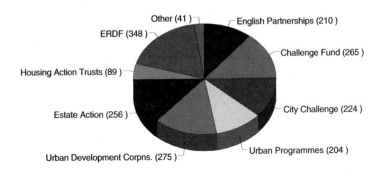

Other (41) — English Partnerships (210) — Challenge Fund (265) — ERDF (348) — Housing Action Trusts (89) — City Challenge (224) — Estate Action (256) — Urban Development Corpns. (275) — Urban Programmes (204)

make the programmes more responsive to local priorities. The current level of the SRB is £1,320 million but the chart also includes programmes for other parts of the UK.

English Partnerships

These non-departmental public bodies (NDPBs) are set up by the Urban Regeneration Agency to encourage the development of new industrial and commercial sites, mainly on derelict land. Based in six regional offices they administer the English Partnerships Investment Fund, which subsidises redevelopment to make it economically viable for private sector developers. The Fund can provide loans and guarantees as well as grants.

Most of the spending - nearly £130 million - is through the Partnership Investment Programme in which private sector developers are involved. This aims to lever in around £400 million of private investment a year. The remaining £50 million available to the Fund is spent on the Land Reclamation Programme and the Direct Development Programme, which provides business premises in areas where development partners cannot be found.

In Wales, the Welsh Development Agency (see Chapter 6) fulfils a similar property development role.

The Challenge Fund

This is so named because allocations are made to projects on the basis of competitive bidding by their sponsors. Introduced in 1995-96, it will become the main method of central government funding of regeneration projects, with its expenditure planned to rise to £600 million in 1998-99.

Schemes must be proposed by local partnerships, usually involving the local authority and the relevant TEC together with other partners drawn from business and voluntary/community sectors. They can last for up to seven years. Just over half of the 329 bids submitted in 1995 received funding, these winning schemes usually addressing several objectives such as housing, employment, enterprise and crime prevention. The partners, particularly the private sector, are committed to put in several times the funding provided by the Fund.

Government Offices for the Regions (GOs)

These were established in 1994 at the same time as the various urban programmes were brought together into the SRB, by combining the regional offices of the Departments for Environment, Trade & Industry, Employment and Transport, which continue to jointly staff the Offices. They aim to foster development of their regions through working with local authorities, TECs and businesses to achieve shared objectives of prosperity and quality of life. The principal offices are located as follows:

Region	Location
North East	Newcastle upon Tyne
North West	Manchester
Yorkshire and Humberside	Leeds
Merseyside	Liverpool
West Midlands	Birmingham
East Midlands	Nottingham
Eastern	Cambridge and Bedford
South West	Bristol and Plymouth
South East	Guildford
London	London

The GOs administer the SRB and also grants from the European Regional Development Fund, helping project sponsors to find the necessary matching funding (usually about 50 per cent).

Government Offices for the Regions (GOs)

City Challenge

This is essentially an earlier, fixed-timescale, fixed-funding, version of the Challenge Fund. It provides £37.5 million to each of 31 five-year Action Plans drawn up by local authorities to revitalise deprived areas, by creating more jobs and making them better places to live and work in. The partnerships between local authorities and others were selected from bids made in 1992 and 1993 and so will complete in 1997 and 1998. The total programme will then have cost just over £1 billion and, it is hoped, will have provided or preserved about 150,000 jobs, reclaimed 3,000 ha of derelict land and constructed or improved over 80,000 dwellings.

City Challenge was itself the successor in England to the Urban Programme, whose final projects complete in 1996-97.

The Urban Programme

Although now almost fully superseded in England, projects in Priority Partnership areas in Scotland may receive funding of £64 million in 1996-97. But if proposals for some devolution of power go ahead this money will instead come directly under the control of local councils, for regeneration expenditure.

In Wales the Strategic Development Scheme to promote economic, environmental and social development of urban areas using local partnerships has a £52 million budget, while in Northern Ireland Urban Development Grants are aimed at the most run-down areas of Belfast and Londonderry. The former also benefits from the Making Belfast Work programme (£25 million).

Urban Development Corporations

Twelve UDCs were set up in the 1980s with responsibility for stimulating the regeneration of urban areas, through the reclamation of some 16,000 hectares of derelict land and the provision of new housing and commercial/industrial development. They have a limited life and three have already completed their tasks and been wound up. Increasing revenue is being generated by the rest, as the projects mature, but government funding is still provided as follows:

Cardiff Bay	£54m
London Docklands	£55m
Merseyside	£35m
Teesside	£25m
Tyne and Wear	£24m
Trafford Park	£22m
Black Country	£20m
Plymouth	£9m
Sheffield	£8m
Birmingham Heartlands	£8m

The last UDCs are due to be wound up by March 1998.

In addition to the above, the Docklands Light Railway, owned by London Docklands UDC until being franchised in 1996 to a private operator, is receiving £20 million government support in 1996-97. Included in this and the Docklands funding is £5 million for repairs arising from the South Quay bomb in February 1996.

Estate Action

Between 1990 and 1995 over 600 Estate Action schemes were set up, with local authorities again competing for funding, but this time specifically for particular run-down housing estates rather than areas of general decay. No new schemes have being started since 1995, and as most have a life of only around two years, the cost of the programme is declining rapidly. Over one hundred schemes involving varying degrees of improvement to around 30,000 council homes will be carried out this year.

The Urban Partnership Initiative in Scotland has similar aims, directed at estates around Glasgow, Edinburgh and Paisley. £33 million is being spent, by Scottish Homes and local authorities.

Housing Action Trusts

These are NDPBs that aim to improve council estates - but in this case by taking them out of the control of their local authorities. On the basis of ballots of residents they have taken over management of the properties and seek to improve them, thus encouraging their purchase by tenants. Up to 20,000 existing houses are affected and some of the Trusts are building new ones. With major building, demolition, renovation and incentive schemes for tenant or housing association purchase, the following levels of government support are in most cases several times the rent income:

Castle Vale (Birmingham)	£14m
Liverpool	£20m
North Hull	£17m
Stonebridge (London Borough of Brent)	£6m
Tower Hamlets	£10m
Waltham Forest	£23m

European Regional Development Fund

The ERDF provides capital support (of up to 50 per cent) for around 2000 regeneration projects being carried out in eligible disadvantaged areas.

The £184 million total ERDF provision for which the DoE is responsible is mainly to support projects in the West Midlands and the north of England. Within each region the Government Office allocates funding to qualifying schemes, mainly sponsored by local authorities and usually receiving matching funding from one of the above government programmes.

Northern Ireland's ERDF grants are worth about £90 million, Scotland's £50 million and Wales' £35 million.

Because ERDF funds are only provided *after* the expenditure has been incurred, the government first grants local authorities Supplementary Credit Approvals to borrow the money for their schemes. When the money is received from Brussels it is used to pay off the debt.

Other

Regional Enterprise Grants, about £15 million a year, help small businesses in qualifying areas invest to create new jobs.

The SRB includes the urban element of the Section 11 grants that pay for linguistic and cultural help for members of ethnic minorities. It was cut from £65 million to £37 million in 1995-96 but its funding for 1996-97 has not been disclosed.

The Groundwork Foundation co-ordinates the work of 43 Groundwork Trusts, working in towns with local authorities and the community to improve the local environment. They plant about 800,000 trees a year, develop footpaths etc. and receive a grant of £7 million. Environmental education is also achieved, through the involvement of over 100,000 schoolchildren a year.

Further Information

Department of the Environment Annual Report 1996. Cm 3207, HMSO. Includes a comprehensive bibliography.

Serving Scotland's Needs. Departments of the Secretary of State for Scotland, and the Forestry Commission. The Government's Expenditure Plans 1996-97 to 1998-99. Cm 3214, HMSO.

Welsh Office Departmental Report 1996. The Government's Expenditure Plans 1996-97 to 1998-99. Cm 3215, HMSO.

Northern Ireland Expenditure Plans and Priorities. The Government's Expenditure Plans 1996-97 to 1998-99. Cm 3216, HMSO.

Housing: Our future Homes. The Government's Housing Policies for England and Wales. Department of the Environment and Welsh Office. Cm 2901, HMSO.

Many programmes dealt with in other chapters have a co-lateral impact on the environment, and the government is now claiming to carry out environmental impact assessments wherever appropriate, e.g. on road projects. But here we bring together a diverse collection of activities whose *main* concern is with the environment - controlling it and protecting it, either for our own benefit or, perhaps in some cases, for its own sake.

Environmental Management
1996-97: £3,730 million

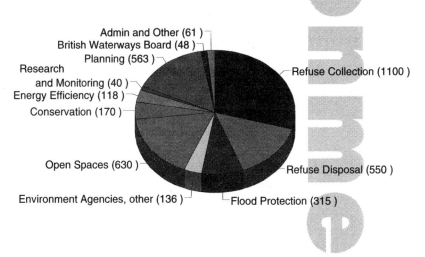

Admin and Other (61)
British Waterways Board (48)
Planning (563)
Research and Monitoring (40)
Energy Efficiency (118)
Conservation (170)
Refuse Collection (1100)
Open Spaces (630)
Refuse Disposal (550)
Environment Agencies, other (136)
Flood Protection (315)

Refuse Collection and Disposal

English district councils are responsible for refuse collection and county councils for disposal, but otherwise (i.e. in the metropolitan districts, Scotland, Wales and Northern Ireland) the functions are combined. The figures shown are only approximate because data published on local authority spending are incomplete and two years out of date. Most of the cost shown for collection relates to the domestic collection service but about £300 million is the cost of street cleaning and litter collection.

Information on the quantities of waste involved is still less accurate because most waste is not weighed, and then a large proportion of local authorities do not respond to the surveys conducted by the Chartered Institute of Public Finance and Accountancy (CIPFA). But the approximate total collected in the UK is 18 million tonnes a year, about 80 per cent of which is domestic waste.

About half of all household waste is recyclable. Government legislation requires that half of this, i.e. 25 per cent of the total, *is* recycled by the year 2000. In 1993-94 the proportion was only 5.5 per cent.

In 1993-94 about 90 per cent of waste was disposed of in landfill but with such sites getting fewer, and with the new landfill tax making them more expensive, other methods, especially incineration, are being used increasingly.

Flood Protection

MAFF and the territorial agriculture departments operate schemes for flood protection and coastal defences. In England, MAFF grants of about £70 million a year are given, to provide on average about half of the cost of capital schemes proposed by local operating authorities - local authorities, the Environment Agency and Internal Drainage Boards. Local authorities borrow about £14 million towards the costs of their schemes as well as paying £186 million in levies to the Environment Agency for its own flood defence spending.

The Environment Agency for England and Wales and the Scottish Environmental Protection Agency

Set up in April 1996, these agencies bring together various functions relating to environmental protection, management and enhancement. They replace the National Rivers Authority (itself only created in 1988 by taking over the water resource management functions of the English and Welsh Water Authorities), the (Scottish) River Purification Authorities, Her Majesty's Inspectorate of Pollution and the local authority waste regulators.

The Environment Agency employs 8,000 people and sees its role as four-fold:

- enforcing regulations and prosecuting offenders
- encouraging prevention and minimisation of waste
- educating and informing the public and industry
- influencing UK and EC policy, based on "sound science"

The Environment Agency

Other Environment Agency Spending

All of the Agency's £76 million spending on water resource management and much of its other non-flood protection spending is financed by charges, but the DoE provides £114 million support as follows:

	DoE support	Total Spending
Pollution control	£80m	£163m
Conservation	£3m	£3m
Navigation	£2m	£6m
Recreation	£1m	£2m
Pensions	£13m	£13m
Setting-up costs	£15m	£15m

The Scottish Environmental Protection Agency receives £22 millon in central government support, for similar activities.

Open Spaces

Most of the £630 million is local authority spending on parks and other open spaces but also included is £17 million for the National Parks (plus the Broads Authority) and £2 million for the National Forest Company.

Local authorities are increasingly contracting out the maintenance of their parks to private companies. In the largest contract of its kind Birmingham City Council transferred 380 staff to Brophy plc, to whom it now pays £10 million a year for the service.

The National Parks are responsible for promoting the enjoyment of the parks by the public, as well as for their conservation. They manage a total of 280,000 hectares although, as much of this is farm land, the 3.3 million visitors a year only have full access to 33,000 hectares. In April 1997 the National Park Boards and Committees are to be replaced by National Park Authorities, within the local government framework.

The government-owned National Forest Company was set up in 1995 to develop a national forest in the East Midlands, through providing grants to landowners and others. It aims to stimulate the planting of 5-600 hectares in 1996-97 and nearly 800 hectares the following year.

Conservation

Nature conservation, particularly through the national nature reserves and Sites of Special Scientific Interest (SSSIs), is the responsibility of English Nature (£39 million), the Countryside Council for Wales (£22 million) and Scottish Natural Heritage (£37 million). These are the successors to the Nature Conservancy Council, which covered the whole of Great Britain until 1991.

They are coordinated by - and fund - the Joint Nature Conservation Committee which is responsible for Britain-wide and international conservation matters, including the EC Habitats Directive, the Convention on International Trade in Endangered Species (CITES) and the UK's Biodiversity Action Plan. The latter was published in 1994, setting out broad strategies, and was followed in December 1995 by a set of detailed recommendations for the conservation of 116 species and 14 key habitats.

English Nature has reduced the number of SSSIs actively monitored from 200, in 1995, to 150, although it has at the same time extended its Wildlife Enhancement Scheme by 2,000 hectares to cover 11,500 hectares. This scheme compensates farmers who forego operations that would be harmful to wildlife.

The 'softer', landscape, aspects of conservation are handled by the same organisations in Scotland and Wales but by the Countryside Commission in England. The latter receives funding of £42 million.

All conservation interests in Northern Ireland are the responsibility of the Environment Service of the province's Department of the Environment (£23 million).

In addition to the expenditure covered here, some measures to improve or protect the environment that relate to agricultural areas are partly funded by the EC's Common Agricultural Policy, or by the agriculture departments, see Chapter 13.

Energy Efficiency

As a nation we spend £50 billion a year on energy, 20 per cent of which could be saved by more efficient use, according to the DoE's Environment and Energy Management Directorate. Its largest programme to reduce this is the Home Energy Efficiency Scheme, which provides grants for low-income households to install insulation. In 1996-97, 415,000 homes of poorer families and the elderly are being treated - a substantial reduction from the 600,000 treated in 1995-96, at a cost of £87 million. The extension of the scheme to all pensioners and disabled people was made in 1994 to partially offset the effect of the imposition of VAT on fuel.

£4 million is spent by the DoE directly on information and publicity for the general public, but it also makes a grant of £25 million to the independent Energy Saving Trust for promotion of the efficient use of energy. The Trust runs local Energy Advice Centres and is managed by the National Energy Foundation.

The building and manufacturing industries are targeted with a Best Practice programme of information transfer, costing £16 million a year, that hopes to achieve annual savings of £800 million (1990 prices) by the year 2000.

Research and Monitoring

The DoE spends £30 million on environmental research and monitoring, covering all types of pollution, e.g. air quality, toxic substances and noise, but also more than one third is spent on global problems such as the greenhouse effect.

In addition the Department provides £10 million in support of international work, especially the monitoring and environmental advocacy activities of the United Nations Environment Programme (£4 million) and the ecological research carried out in developing countries under the Darwin Initiative (£3 million).

Planning

The Town and Country Planning Act, 1990, made local authorities responsible for producing development plans within a framework set by DoE's national and regional policy, and codified through its Planning and Policy Guidance (PPG) notes. As well as area-wide plans, local plans must be produced for mineral extraction and waste disposal. Most authorities aim to have completed most of their plans by the end of 1996, although only about a third will have produced their Waste Plans by then.

However it is the day-to-day work of local authority planning departments, working on about 500,000 applications for planning permission a year, that consumes most time and resources. The DoE issues a number of further PPGs providing guidance on dealing with planning applications and sets a national target of 8 weeks for their determination, but some 35 per cent take longer.

The Planning Inspectorate Executive Agency costs £28 million and employs 600 staff dealing with local planning inquiries, appeals against refusal of planning permission, and enforcement appeals.

To inform its planning policies and guidance the DoE commissions research on land use and minerals supply planning issues, at a cost of around £4 million a year.

The British Waterways Board

This nationalised industry is responsible for managing and encouraging the use of our inland waterways, for freight as well as leisure. Its £80 million budget includes £48 million from the Department of the Environment, with the rest generated commercially.

Other

This includes £50 million for the cost of DoE administration and £24 million spending on waste and recycling initiatives, as well as a number of small projects and grants costing less than £5 million each.

Further Information

Department of the Environment Annual Report 1996. Cm 3207, HMSO.

1995 Environment White Paper "This Common Inheritance: UK Annual Report 1995".

Biodiversity Steering Group Report - Vol 1, Meeting the Rio Challenge. HMSO, December 1995.

Waste Collection Statistics, 1993-94 Actuals.   CIPFA 1995

Waste Disposal Statistics, 1993-94 Actuals.   CIPFA 1995

This chapter deals with the cost of crime - of protection against it, of investigating it and of dealing with the perpetrators. The growth in crime since the 1970s has caused law and order to be the fastest growing of all the major expenditure categories, with a doubling in real terms in the last fifteen years.

Law and Order
1996-97: £14.6 billion

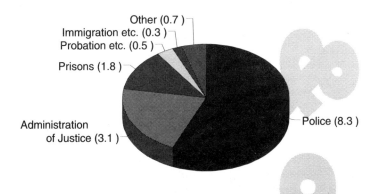

Other (0.7)
Immigration etc. (0.3)
Probation etc. (0.5)
Prisons (1.8)
Administration of Justice (3.1)
Police (8.3)

Spending Trends, 1996-97 prices

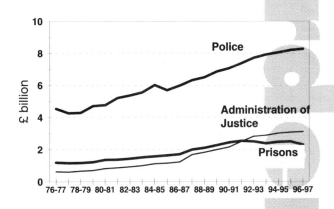

Police

Administration of Justice

Prisons

£ billion

10
8
6
4
2
0

76-77 78-79 80-81 82-83 84-85 86-87 88-89 90-91 92-93 94-95 96-97

Police

The police account for more than half of the total spend. Of the fifty-two separate forces in Britain, the Metropolitan Police alone are directly accountable to the Home Secretary. The 41 others in England and Wales are answerable to local police authorities, composed mainly of county councillors and magistrates. The eight police forces in Scotland correspond to the old Regional Council areas but are now responsible to the new local authorities, while Northern Ireland's Royal Ulster Constabulary comes under the Northern Ireland Office.

Crime Prevention

As well as using their officers' visible presence to deter crime, the police employ about 800 specialist crime prevention officers to advise the public. Substantial money is also spent elsewhere on trying to prevent crime, as follows.

The 'Other' category on the pie chart includes £19 million spent directly by the Home Office but the Ministerial Group on Crime Prevention, representing twelve government departments, estimates that their total expenditure on crime prevention through diverse programmes is of the order of £250 million. The Group aims to supervise the government's broad crime prevention strategy and has set up an Official Group on Crime Prevention to implement it, where appropriate, through Departmental programmes.

In 1995 the National Board for Crime Prevention was replaced by the National Crime Prevention Agency. Its members, from the Home Office, police authorities, the Association of Chief Police Officers and business, are charged with developing a crime prevention strategy.

The value of Closed Circuit Television in reducing crime has been well demonstrated in Bradford, Newcastle and elsewhere. Expanding on its earlier support, the government is offering £15 million in 1996-97 to help fund new CCTV schemes. Awards will be made on a competitive basis, according to the merits of individual schemes and the finance provided by other parties. This should permit the introduction of some 3,000 cameras in 300 new schemes. The government is also committed to a similar level of finance for the following two years.

In a good example of improving public accountability, the government requires police authorities to provide council tax payers with details of their finances and spending. So we all have access to these details for our local forces.

Spending is dominated, of course, by pay and pensions. There are just over 150,000 police officers in the UK supported by an increasing number of civilians (currently about 60,000) taking over the administrative work to release more officers for front-line duties. The government is pledged to make available extra funds to increase the number of police officers by 5,000, i.e. 3 per cent, over the next three years.

Through the 1994 Police and Magistrates' Courts Act the government took control of police spending in England and Wales. Previously the Home Office had reimbursed 51 per cent of whatever local authorities decided to spend on policing; now it pays to each police authority 51 per cent of a figure that it decides they need, leaving local authorities to fund the rest. The extra funding to allow for the recruitment mentioned above is £20 million in 1996-97, rising to £100 million in 1998-99.

One cost of the troubles in Northern Ireland is much of the £630 million bill for the Royal Ulster Constabulary, with 8,500 full-time officers and 4,700 in the RUC reserve. A successful conclusion of the peace process could lead to manpower being halved, saving around £250 million a year.

The Home Office Police Department provides central services to the constabularies, for about £150 million. These services include training (£45 million), the Police National Computer and the National Criminal Intelligence Service (£30 million). The NCIS coordinates work between police forces, as is frequently necessary in anti-drugs work for example, and is the main contact with Interpol and the new Europol. It has recently started to make use of Security Service staff in the fight against serious crime.

The Police Department also spends nearly £40 million on formulating and implementing government policies on efficient policing. This includes the operation of HM Inspectorate of Constabulary which inspects and publishes reports on all constabularies in England and Wales, and the RUC, each year.

Administration of Justice
1996-97: £3,120 million

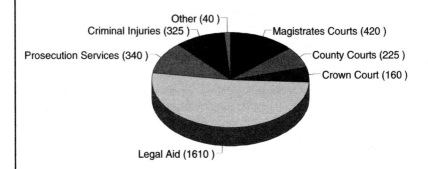

Other (40)
Criminal Injuries (325)
Magistrates Courts (420)
Prosecution Services (340)
County Courts (225)
Crown Court (160)
Legal Aid (1610)

England and Wales, Scotland, and Northern Ireland have their own legal systems, with considerable differences in law, organisation and practice. For simplicity, the courts shown in the pie chart relate to the system in England and Wales but the costs include those of their equivalents in Scotland and Northern Ireland.

The Courts
The most serious crimes, such as rape and murder, are tried in the high court - the Crown Court in England, Wales and Northern Ireland, and the High Court of Justiciary in Scotland - by judges and juries. There are about 90,000 such trials a year.

Less criminal serious offences are dealt with in England and Wales by magistrates' courts, presided over mainly by 28,000 unpaid magistrates. In Scotland minor cases are heard by the district courts and cases of intermediate seriousness by the sheriff court, which for some will use a judge and jury.

Magistrates' courts and sheriff courts also deal with the less serious *civil* prosecutions. Others are heard in the 270 county courts in England and Wales and the Court of Session in Scotland. The High Court in England and Wales deals with complex civil cases.

The Court Service, a new agency within the Lord Chancellor's Department, provides administrative support to the higher courts and tribunals and is charged with increasing their efficiency and performance. (A similar new agency administers the courts in Scotland.) The Lord Chancellor's Department also oversees administration of magistrates' courts, is responsible for the Northern Ireland Court Service, and funds the legal aid scheme.

Although magistrates' courts are run by local authorities most of their costs are met by grants from central government.

Legal Aid

Around four million legal aid claims are paid each year. Payments for legal advice make up the majority of claims, but three-quarters of the actual money goes to the costs of civil and criminal trials:

Legal Aid in England and Wales, 1996-97

	Bills paid	Cost
Civil Legal Aid	390,000	£715m
Criminal Legal Aid	800,000	£550m
Advice and assistance	2,850,000	£290m

There have been several notoriously wealthy recipients of legal aid in recent years including an MoD official said to have at least £2 million of bribes in Swiss bank accounts. To try to prevent abuses like this in the future the Lord Chancellor is setting up an investigation unit for carrying out complex means assessments, and the rules themselves have been modified. Any excess value of the claimant's house over £100,000 is now included, as is money owned by family and, in some circumstances, friends.

Prosecution Services

The Crown Prosecution Service (CPS) is a government department responsible to the Attorney General. When the police request a prosecution in England or Wales the CPS carries it through, if it decides that the evidence and the public interest justify it. In Scotland the Lord Advocate, through the Crown Office, has responsibility for all prosecutions. Cases in the lower courts are prepared and prosecuted by procurators fiscal, who also work with Crown Office officials on the preparation of high court cases, which are prosecuted by Crown Counsel (a collective term for the Lord Advocate, the Solicitor General for Scotland and advocates depute).

In Northern Ireland the police still prosecute most minor offences but the Director of Public Prosecutions for Northern Ireland deals with offences tried on indictment.

The relationship between the police and the CPS is not an easy one: CPS performance indicators encourage the dropping of all cases for which there is not a very good chance of conviction, so about 150,000 defendants have all charges dropped each year. This is the main reason why, despite rising crime, the number of convictions is falling.

Because of the very technical nature of fraud, the Serious Fraud Office not only carries out the investigation but also the prosecution, in the most serious and complex cases. It faced substantial criticism over its failure to obtain convictions against the Maxwell brothers in the Mirror Group Pension Fund case. Fraud cases in Scotland are prosecuted by the Crown Office Fraud Unit.

Criminal Injuries Compensation Scheme

This pays out compensation to innocent victims of crime, except in Northern Ireland where there is instead a statutory compensation system. About 83,000 claims are expected in 1996-97 but the numbers are rising by about 6,000 a year.

The scheme pays out more than similar schemes in the rest of Europe put together, and in April 1994 the Home Secretary tried to take steps to control the cost, which had doubled over the previous four years. A new tariff-based system was imposed, awarding standard compensation sums according to the injury suffered, and operated for a year before its method of introduction was judged unlawful. So, after a slowing in its growth, expenditure rose sharply the following year, due in part to the re-assessment of cases settled during 1994-95.

The Criminal Injuries Compensation Act was then passed, to allow the lawful introduction in April 1996 of a modified tariff system, that also takes loss of earnings into account. It is forecast that this will reduce the average cost per claim by 25 per cent.

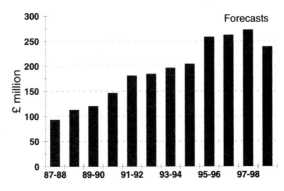

Criminal Injuries Compensation
Great Britain, 1996-97 prices

Forecasts

£ million

300
250
200
150
100
50
0

87-88 89-90 91-92 93-94 95-96 97-98

Prisons

These are run by the Prison Service (in Wales as well as England) and the Scottish and Northern Ireland Prison Services. 70 per cent of the Prison Service's annual budget of about £1600 million is spent on employing 39,000 staff, and its cost per prisoner is about £25,000 a year. In Northern Ireland the latter is about three times as high.

The population of the 30 prisons in England and Wales fell between 1988 and 1992 but has since risen sharply to about 55,000, of which about 15 per cent are on remand:

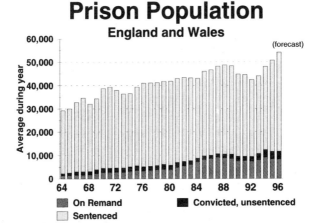

Prison Population
England and Wales

(forecast)

Average during year

60,000
50,000
40,000
30,000
20,000
10,000
0

64 68 72 76 80 84 88 92 96

On Remand   Convicted, unsentenced
Sentenced

Does Prison Work?

The government cites "protecting the public" as the justification for its increasing use of prisons. They certainly carry out this function for as long as offenders are behind bars, but does the threat of prison deter the would-be criminal, and what effect does prison have on the future behaviour of those incarcerated?

The 1990 government White Paper, "Crime, Justice and Protecting the Public" acknowledged that most crime is impulsive and so may not be effectively deterred by sentencing policies, while most "professional" crime escapes any justice. So the deterrent argument does not look very strong.

And can we expect prisons to have a reforming effect on their inmates when they find themselves surrounded by criminal experience and expertise and subject to strong pressure to adopt the values - and often drug habits - of their new peers?

Home Office research has found that to reduce crime by 1 per cent we would need to increase the number of prison places by 25 per cent, at a cost of £1 billion. But even this looks optimistic when the United States has been unable to curb its rising crime rate despite doubling its prison population in the last ten years. In Germany, on the other hand, a 20 per cent reduction in prisoners has led to no increase in crime.

Another 6,000 prisoners are held in Scotland and 2,000 in Northern Ireland.

The growing number of remand prisoners reflects an increased intake, rather than longer delays between arrest and sentencing or release: the average time prisoners are held on remand is fairly static, at about eight weeks.

The Prison Service is looking for ways to cope with the 60,000 prisoners expected by autumn 1997. The current building programme of six new prisons and seventeen prison extensions is still expected to leave a shortfall of 4,000 places. This may be met by refurbishment of mothballed units and further extensions, costing at least £100 million on top of current spending plans.

The government is paying for most of the new building already in progress, costing nearly £300 million a year, but two of the new prisons - Bridgend and Fazakerley - are being privately financed. Whoever pays, the capital cost per new prison place is about £110,000.

Currently four prisons are privately operated, but still within the Prison Service, and are showing cost savings of at least 15 per cent. Bridgend and Fazakerley will also be managed by the private sector and the government's goal is for about ten per cent of all prisons to be privately operated. The two Court Escort and Custody Service areas that have been contracted out have also achieved savings together with, it is claimed, a reduction in escapes.

It is estimated that the proposed introduction of minimum three-year sentences for burglars after their third conviction would increase the prison population by a further 10,000, requiring another twelve prisons.

'Being in Parkhurst is no excuse for not visiting your mother'

The Probation Service

The 55 local authority-run Probation Services in England and Wales supervise offenders undertaking community sentences of from 6 to 36 months, and help them to move towards law-abiding lifestyles.

About 100,000 probation and community service orders are made each year. Probation orders can be used in place of prison and impose varying degrees of restriction on a convicted person's freedom as punishment within the community. They usually also include a requirement to meet regularly with a probation officer and/or attend a day centre to help the individual's rehabilitation.

Community service is similar but involves a specified number of hours (40 to 240) unpaid work to be completed within 12 months. The two orders can now be combined in appropriate cases.

Immigration and Nationality

£220 million is spent each year through the Home Office's Immigration and Nationality Department. About 2,300 of the 5,600 staff are employed on immigration control duties at ports and airports; some 500 others deal with the 175,000 resulting immigration cases.

The department also deals with the cases of people seeking asylum from regimes that might harm them if they returned home. Since a massive increase in the numbers of people seeking asylum in Britain in 1991 (49,000 - four times the number two years earlier) the numbers have now stabilised at 30-40,000 a year. To tackle the large backlog of cases that remains, the department aims to complete at least 45,000 cases in 1996-97.

Also included in this section of the pie chart is the £50 million cost of the Passport Agency.

Further Information

Home Office Annual Report, 1996. Cm 3208, HMSO.

Departmental Report of the Lord Chancellor's and Law Officer's Department. The Government's Expenditure Plans 1996-97 to 1998-99. Cm 3209, HMSO.

Crime and Social Policy, Nacro Publications 1995. 169 Clapham Road, London SW9 OPU.

Criminal Statistics, England and Wales (Annual), Home Office.

Prison Statistics, England and Wales (Annual), Home Office.

11

As medical knowledge grows and new drugs and technologies become available the potential for spending ever more to keep us living ever longer rises indefinitely. But, despite spending increases, the NHS budget will never be able to afford all that is possible for everyone who could benefit, so administrators and clinicians are increasingly under pressure to make difficult decisions on the allocation of limited resources.

One way of saving money costs is to transfer care wherever possible from hospitals to the local social services, also covered in this chapter, where costs per person are lower.

Health and Social Services
1996-97: £52.1 billion

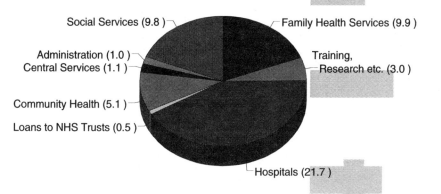

Social Services (9.8)
Family Health Services (9.9)
Administration (1.0)
Central Services (1.1)
Training,
Research etc. (3.0)
Community Health (5.1)
Loans to NHS Trusts (0.5)
Hospitals (21.7)

The NHS comprises all segments except for social services and so totals £42.3 billion. The Department of Health (DoH) funds only England, with the Welsh, Scottish and Northern Ireland Offices each responsible for their own programmes. Social Services are run by local authorities, except in Northern Ireland where there is a combined government department of Health and Social Services.

The following graph demonstrates how expenditure in both areas has grown - in real terms - since 1978, and how social services spending has doubled in the last ten years:

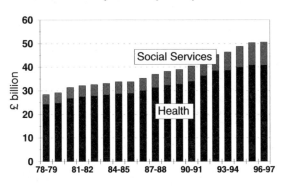

Health and Social Services Growth
(1996-97 prices)

Family Health Services (FHS)

The costs of the four family health services, with all drugs shown under pharmaceutical services rather than with the doctors that prescribe them, are as follows:

Family Health Services
1996-97: £9.9 billion

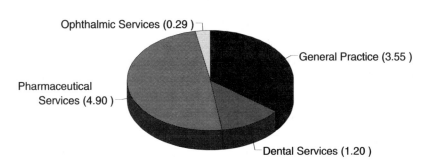

General Practitioners (GPs), dentists, pharmacists and ophthalmologists are self-employed, so much FHS spending depends upon the performance-related pay formulae contained in the contracts introduced in 1990.

General Practice

There are now 32,000 GPs in Britain, employing about 60,000 staff including over 10,000 practice nurses, and carrying out 250-300 million consultations a year.

The costs of general practice (known officially as general medical services) are split administratively between the £2,500 million non-cash-limited budget and the £1,050 million cash-limited, for staff, improvements to premises, computers and the Practice Fundholders Management Allowance.

GP Fundholding

About 55 per cent of the population are now served by GP practices who have chosen to manage NHS funds themselves. Their budgets must pay for their staff, hospital referrals, community nursing services and management costs. Prescriptions are also charged to their fund, encouraging the prescribing of the cheaper versions of drugs, but also potentially discouraging some practices from accepting "expensive" patients onto their lists.

Fundholders negotiate with NHS trusts for levels and costs of services to be provided each year. These contracts give the fundholders prior claims on the services' resources, sometimes resulting in longer waiting times for the patients of other practices. Conversely, some fundholders run out of money towards the end of the financial year; then *their* patients have to wait.

Dental Services

The cost shown is net of Dental charges of some £500 million - 30 per cent of the full costs - and excludes, of course, the costs and charges of private dentistry.

The remuneration of Britain's 18,500 dentists has been the source of much conflict between the profession and government over the last five years. After the introduction of a new contract, dentists were overpaid in 1991-92 because of underestimates of the work they would carry out. The government reduced payments the following year leading to many dentists ceasing NHS work, at least for adults.

The NHS pays dentists by item of service and recovers 80 per cent of the cost from the patient, unless they are eligible for free treatment. Many or most dentists are now only providing NHS treatment to those to whom it is free, and treating others privately. This is why the income to the NHS from charges is so low, compared with the standard 80 per cent level.

In areas where it is now difficult to obtain NHS treatment the Community Dental Service (see Community Health Services, below) is having to be strengthened.

Smoking

With both hospitals and general practitioners increasingly being forced to make hard choices about priorities, a debate has arisen over whether people who are responsible for their condition should be treated the same as those who are sick through no fault of their own.

The government has estimated that smoking-related diseases cost the NHS about £500 million a year and industry about £2 billion through 30 million lost working days. Government policy is to discourage smoking by health education, and to reduce it from the current 26 per cent to 20 per cent by the year 2000. But this will not benefit the government's balance sheet – it gains about £8.5 billion a year from taxes on tobacco (see Chapter 18). So smokers could certainly argue that they have paid for whatever treatment their addiction leads to.

Pharmaceutical Services

The NHS has 9,800 contracting pharmacies in England. The £4.9 billion is the net cost for the UK, after subtraction of about £350 million income from prescription charges. The drugs themselves cost £4 billion while the dispensing costs, for staff, premises etc., are about £850 million.

Over 540 million prescriptions are dispensed each year, at an average net cost of about £9, and both the number and the unit cost are increasing. So total costs are rising at about five per cent, or £150-200 million a year, in real terms. The Audit Commission estimated in March 1994 that a reduction of nearly £0.5 billion could be achieved by "a more rational approach to prescribing". For example it is estimated that the £400 million spent on antibiotics could be halved by stopping prescribing them for colds and 'flu, for which they can do nothing. The government is now taking a number of measures to encourage more cost-effective prescribing.

Many prescribed drugs are also available "over the counter" at a lower cost than the prescription charge but, because GPs are obliged when recommending treatment to make out a prescription, patients often pay more for their treatment than if they had bought it directly.

Ophthalmic Services

There about 7,500 ophthalmic opticians and optometrists practising in Britain. The 1989 restriction on free eye tests more than halved the number paid for by the NHS, to about 4.5 million a year. But since then there has been an increase, as more people have become eligible, to over 8 million free tests a year, resulting in the NHS paying for over 4 million prescriptions.

Training, Research, etc.

Most funding for Hospital and Community Health Services (HCHS) is distributed to Health Authorities, for direct purchase of care from Trusts or for use by fundholding practices to pay for Trusts' treatment of their patients. But about £3 billion is taken in national levies, largely for the education and training of doctors and dentists (£970 million) and nurses, midwives and other professional groups (£790 million).

About £450 million is levied for hospitals' research and the remaining £0.5 billion pays for various common national services, including provision for medical negligence claims (about £90 million).

Hospitals

There are about 1600 hospitals in Britain. Most are District General Hospitals but about £30 million is spent on specialist hospitals outside the Health Authority system, such as Great Ormond Street and the Brompton Heart and Chest Hospital.

To limit the rate at which costs are rising, hospitals try to minimise the time patients spend on the wards and wherever possible treat them as outpatients. Between 1990 and 1994 (the last year for which data are available) the number of outpatients increased by 22 per cent.

The following chart is an estimate of the current pattern and levels of all hospital spending, estimated on the basis of 1993-94 data for England. Separate figures for inpatients and outpatients are not available.

Hospitals
1996-97: £21.7 billion

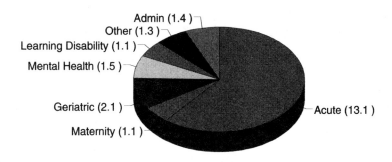

Given the current total cost of treating acute illnesses and injuries, the reduction in average stay from over ten days in 1984 to about six for these cases, has saved of the order of £5 billion a year.

Public spending on hospital building in 1996-97 is down about £260 million, or 14 per cent, in favour of letting contracts under the Private Finance Initiative (PFI). The first such scheme to get off the ground was the £35 million modernisation of the South Buckinghamshire NHS Trust's two hospitals at High Wycombe and Amersham. Hospitals built under the PFI will continue to be maintained by the private sector while being leased to NHS Trusts.

Health Service Reorganisation

England's 14 regional health authorities were replaced in April 1996 by eight regional offices of the NHS Executive. At the same time, the 105 district health authorities that had held responsibility for hospitals, and the 90 family health service authorities (FHSAs) that funded general practitioners and dentists, were re-structured into 100 unified Health Authorities. With increasing hospital funding coming from the FHSAs through fundholding general practitioners, the old functional split had become an anachronism.

The government hopes that the new authorities will be able to take a more strategic approach to the development of health provision in their area, working with community health services and local authorities as well as with GPs and hospitals. They will promote the extension of fundholding in order to make the NHS increasingly primary care led, and also be responsible for provision of public health advice.

It is intended that the restructuring will reduce the £1 billion a year spending on administration and other overheads by about £150 million, by 1997-98.

NHS Trusts

All hospitals and other health service units, such as ambulance services and community and mental health services, are now run as self-governing NHS Trusts. There are about 440 in England. Instead of receiving Health Authority money as required (subject to the authority's budget) they obtain their income through contracts with their authority and with GP fundholders.

The main pie chart shows the £473 million that the government is lending to Trusts for capital spending, to supplement any funds of their own derived from charging (and thus contained within the costs shown for the services provided by the Trusts).

Because the Trusts are managed as businesses they are required to generate a six per cent return on their assets, most of which is used to pay interest and 'Public Dividend Capital' dividends to the government. So the government is getting back as 'income' about £1 billion of the £27 billion that the Trusts are charging in 1996-97.

Hospitals and the Elderly

A rising proportion of old people in the population is putting increasing pressure on the resources of the NHS. The average annual cost of people aged over 84 is about £2,500 a year, compared with about £1,400 for those aged 75 to 84.

At the current rate of demographic change this creates an increase of nearly 1 per cent a year in demand. So hospitals are trying to minimise the length of time patients spend in geriatric wards and have reduced the average from over fifty days in 1984 to less than twenty. But over the same period admissions have grown by 60 per cent. The two may, of course, be connected.

Community Health

This covers the provision by the NHS of various medical services to people where they live, rather than in hospital. Our estimates of costs are again extrapolated from England's for 1994-95, and so are only approximate:

Community Health Services
1996-97: £5.1 billion

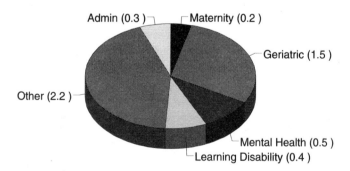

'Other' costs include family planning advice, immunisation, screening, health promotion, community dental services and others.

Health visitors, physiotherapists and district nurses account for most of the visits carried out, each visiting of the order of five million people a year. Just over a million people receive help from the community dental service.

Central Services

The £1.1 billion shown for central services on the main pei chart includes £500 million of support for the NHS Pension Scheme.

Of the £600 million of true 'services', £125 million reimburses other EC states for their treatment of UK nationals and some £60 million provides grants to national voluntary organisations working within the field of health and social services, but most of the costs are associated with public health.

The Department of Health tries to promote and protect public health through developing and implementing a number of specific policies. Most of the scientific support for these is provided by the Public Health Laboratory Service (£100 million), National Radiological Protection Board (£14 million), the Centre for Applied Microbiology and Research (£6 million) and the National Biological Standards Board (£9 million).

£170 million provides free milk to young families on income support and to children in nurseries.

Various information services cost about £50 million and include the health promotion budget. Health promotion services are being opened up to competitive tender, rather than being carried out, as in the past, solely through the Health Education Authority.

Administration and Management

The £1 billion shown includes about £350 million for central government departments and an estimate of £700 million for the Health Authorities.

At one time the NHS was regarded as under-managed, but the formation of the internal market has been criticised for creating large numbers of managerial jobs. So the management budgets of Health Authorities and NHS Trusts are being cut in 1996-97 by five per cent from the previous year's levels - a reduction of about eight per cent in real terms. This will be helped by the rationalising of the regional tier of management and the combining of the Family Health and Hospital and Community Health functions (see box on Health Service Reorganisation).

Social Services

While the NHS broadly aims to improve people's health by appropriate treatment, the permanently sick, the aged and the disabled are helped by the Personal Social Services. These are provided mainly by local authorities, but in Northern Ireland by central government.

Since 1993-94 the Department of Health has been ratcheting up the resources of English local authorities through a special transitional grant for community care. The cumulative effect by 1996-97, the final year of transition, is an additional £2.4 billion a year, which will now be consolidated into the normal Revenue Support Grant calculations for future years. The DoH stipulates that at least 85 per cent of the new money is spent on buying provision from the private sector. This accelerates the trend of local authorities shifting from being providers of services to purchasers.

Although the total level of spending for 1996-97 can be estimated with reasonable confidence, the allocation of net costs (for some services there are significant payments from clients) is imprecise. The following pie chart shows our best estimates but should, therefore, be treated with some caution:

Personal Social Services
1996-97: £9.8 billion

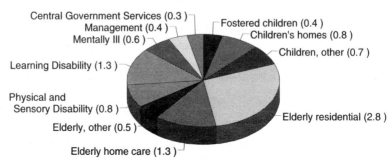

Central Government Services (0.3)
Management (0.4)
Mentally Ill (0.6)
Fostered children (0.4)
Children's homes (0.8)
Children, other (0.7)
Learning Disability (1.3)
Physical and Sensory Disability (0.8)
Elderly, other (0.5)
Elderly residential (2.8)
Elderly home care (1.3)

Children

About 45,000 children are fostered, at a cost of about £8,000 each per year, while children's homes are still needed for nearly 15,000 - far less satisfactory and costing around £45,000 for each place. About 40 per cent of the children are in homes run by voluntary and private groups.

There has been an effort in recent years to remove children from their families only as a last resort, resulting in an increase in social work costs to support them and monitor their development at home.

The Elderly

Care for the elderly accounts for half of the social services budget. Residential care, at about £300 a week, is provided for 170,000 people, while about 50,000 attend day centres and clubs each day. The 1996-97 increase in the capital limits for the residential means test reduced clients' contributions to costs, requiring an additional £70 million of government support to local authorities.

The Department of Health has a policy of facilitating independent living for the elderly, and so encourages the expansion of the relevant domiciliary services provided by local authorities, providing help to about 700,000 people a week.

Physical and Sensory Disabilities

Nearly £200 million provides residential care for the 10,000 or so most handicapped people, with 80 per cent of it in the voluntary and private sectors. Another 15,000 people attend day centres, costing around £100 million. Specific equipment and adaptations to help individuals to cope with their disability cost another £100 million.

Over a quarter of costs for this group are reported as 'other', which includes funding for various organisations providing advice and a variety of forms of help and support.

People with Learning Disabilities

Roughly half of the total cost is on residential care for around 30,000 people, with a unit cost higher than for the elderly, at about £360 a week. The rest is spent on day centres and social education for about 70,000 people, provided almost entirely by the local authorities themselves.

The Mentally Ill

Since 1990 there has been a large shift in the provision for the mentally ill. Large NHS hospitals used to provide about 80,000 beds but most have now been closed with the responsibility for care transferring largely to local authorities and private and voluntary providers. Local authorities now provide some 6,000 residential places themselves, and pay the voluntary and private sectors to provide a further 20,000. Day centres specifically for the mentally ill host about 12,000 clients a day, and cost £100 a week per place.

A large proportion of local health authorities do not yet have comprehensive strategies for community care of the mentally ill, and complain of inadequate resources. In February 1996 the government accepted the problems and announced proposals for some 400 new homes for 5-10,000 of the most disturbed patients. But while an additional £95 million has been allocated to mental health services in 1996-97, the homes are expected to cost £400 million to build and £250 million a year to run.

Further Information

Department of Health Departmental Report. The Government's Expenditure Plans 1996-97 to 1998-99. Cm 3212, HMSO.

Personal Social Services Statistics, 1995-96 Estimates. CIPFA.

Health and Personal Social Services Statistics for England. Department of Health, HMSO.

As by far the largest area of public expenditure, Social Security has been the main focus of the government's attack on the budget deficit. It is also of course a very political arena, where people's views of the merit of particular benefits can be strongly coloured by their whole view of the way society should work.

Social Security
1996-97: £96.6 billion

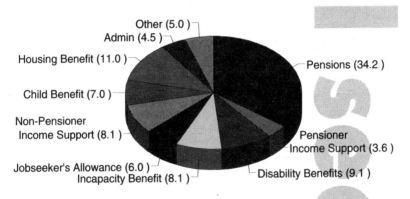

Other (5.0)
Admin (4.5)
Housing Benefit (11.0)
Child Benefit (7.0)
Non-Pensioner
Income Support (8.1)
Jobseeker's Allowance (6.0)
Incapacity Benefit (8.1)
Pensions (34.2)
Pensioner
Income Support (3.6)
Disability Benefits (9.1)

Pensions account for a third of the total, with Income Support (shown here in two parts, but totalling £11.5 billion) the next largest, but a long way behind.

Pensions

£28 billion of the pensions total is the basic retirement pension so this alone represents nearly 10 per cent of total government spending. There are 10.5 million recipients, single people receiving £61 a week and retired couples £98.

At present, women - if they have paid sufficient National Insurance contributions - qualify at 60, and men at 65, but the government has determined that from the year 2020 pensionable age will be equalised at 65. If this were the case now, about one and a half million fewer women would be receiving the pension and payments would be £3.5 billion lower.

Two other relatively small pensions are included in the £34 billion - the State Earnings-Related Pensions Scheme (SERPS) costing £3 billion, and war pension £1.4 billion. The discretionary Christmas Bonus paid to all pensioners costs about £135 million each year.

The Job Seeker's Allowance

Currently, Unemployment Benefit is paid at £46.45 a week for single people and £75.10 for married couples, for just the first six months of a period of unemployment. If still unemployed after that time, people then claim Income Support. In October 1996 this system is being replaced by the Job Seeker's Allowance, which retains the same two-stage treatment.

A contributions-based allowance is paid for the first six months, at the same rate as the old Unemployment Benefit. Thereafter, the allowance is based on need rather than past National Insurance contributions, with an age-related allowance supplemented by payments for dependent children and mortgage interest. The main difference from the old system is that claimants have to enter into a Job Seeker's Agreement which will continue as long as they claim the allowance. This agreement identifies the steps the claimant will take to find work, and how the Employment Office will help.

The DSS hopes to achieve a reduction of £60 million in 1996-97 and £240 million in 1997-98, through implementation of the new system.

The Cost of Unemployment

The Job Seeker's Allowance provides a clear minimum measure, £6.0 billion, of the cost of unemployment. But this does not take account of other benefits paid to unemployed people, nor the cost of benefits paid to people who would work if the right sort of work was available but who do not need to claim Job Seeker's Allowance because they are already eligible for another benefit. The government estimates that including the first of these, mainly Housing Benefit paid to the unemployed, brings the cost to £8.4 billion.

A second approach, that tries to include also the benefits to people who do not need to register as unemployed, is to look at changes in the level of "cyclic" social security. So-named because it rises and falls with the economic cycle, this includes the cost of Income Support to all people of working age, as well as the cost of the Job Seeker's Allowance.

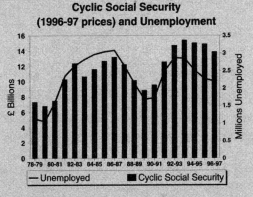

Cyclic Social Security (1996-97 prices) and Unemployment

The trends of cyclic social security and unemployment match quite well, but with a steady increase in the ratio of the former to the latter since 1983-84. This could indicate that - with the growth of training schemes and part-time working - unemployment numbers are an increasingly poor measure of the shortage of work. But, taking the numbers as given, an increase in unemployment of one million between 1990-91 and 1992-93 was accompanied by a £5 billion increase in payments. If we extrapolate to the current 2.2 million level, we get an estimate of around £11 billion that implicitly takes account of Income Support to people who are not on the unemployment register. The addition of unemployment-related Housing Benefit takes the estimate to £13 billion.

To these estimates of the cost of benefits could be added the £1 billion in allowances paid to people on Youth Training and Modern Apprenticeships schemes, who employers would mostly train at their own expense in times of labour shortages.

The National Insurance Fund

Entitlement to some social security benefits - notably Retirement Pension, Incapacity Benefit and Jobseeker's Allowance during the first six months of unemployment - depends upon an individual's past record of National Insurance (NI) contributions. These contributory benefits are paid from the National Insurance Fund and make up half of the value of all benefit payments - about £45 billion.

The "Fund" is in fact run as a simple current account, with the government trying to keep income and outgoings in line, while holding very small balances. Rates of NI contributions have in the past been set such that the income from them substantially exceeded the cost of benefit payments, and the surplus has been used for other purposes - nominally for NHS funding. Between 9 and 17 per cent was used thus during the '80s, depending on the levels of NI receipts. The latest basis for the diversion is enshrined in the Social Security Administration Act, 1992, which allows about 12 per cent of contributions to be used for the NHS.

But the Fund's expenditure rose sharply in the early '90s, necessitating a subsidy from the government's consolidated fund.

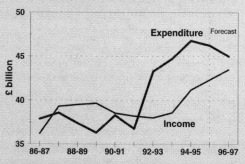

National Insurance Fund
Income and Expenditure, 1996-97 prices

So although the £47 billion expected in "National Insurance" contributions in 1996-97 still exceeds the cost of benefits, the Fund needs a subsidy of around £4 billion because nearly £6 billion goes to the NHS.

Incapacity Benefit

This replaced Invalidity and Sickness benefits in 1995 in an effort to reduce spending. The number of Invalidity Benefit claimants had doubled over the previous ten years to about 1.8 million, until the benefit cost £8 billion. Eligibility criteria are now tighter and more formal medical tests are required. The following graph shows the effect on spending - the government expects a saving of £1.2 billion in 1996-97.

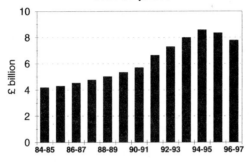

Incapacity Benefits
1996-97 prices

(Excludes Statutory Sick Pay, paid by the government until 1994-95 and then by employers)

But many people no longer eligible for the benefit have now moved to Income Support/Job Seeker's Allowance.

Incapacity Benefit has three rates, according to the duration of the period of incapacity, with the maximum for a single person being £61 a week.

Council Tax Benefit

Council Tax Benefit

This is not included in the Social Security spending total because government regards it not as spending but as a loss of tax income. The cost of the benefit in 1996-97 is £2 billion, and there are six million recipients.

Disability Benefits

There are several of these. The following table shows the numbers of recipients and the money involved in 1996-97:

	'000s people	£ billion
Disability Living Allowance	2,000	4.4
Attendance Allowance	1,250	2.4
Severe Disablement Allowance	380	0.9
Invalid Care Allowance	400	0.8

The Disability Living Allowance is paid to those who became disabled before the age of 65, and has separate components for care and mobility. The top rates are £48.50 and £33.90 a week respectively, and the lowest is £12.90 for each. The top mobility rate can be used to lease cars from the Motability charity, which receives £4 million towards its administration costs from the DSS.

Attendance Allowance, for the elderly disabled, also has two rates according to the degree of help required - £48.50 and £32.40.

As well as the main benefits tabulated above, there is also a Disability Working Allowance to help people who are able to work to a limited extent. But take-up has been less than expected so the cost is only £25m.

Income Support

This is paid at different rates according to circumstances, for example a family with one child under 11 and another between 11 and 15 receives £126.30 a week. There are four million recipients - people with little money and working 16 hours a week or less, or not at all.

Income Support also pays some or all of the mortgage interest of owner occupiers, representing some £1.1 billion. The government has recently introduced new rules and limits to curb this expenditure and to encourage people to take out private mortgage insurance instead of relying on a state safety net. Those with mortgages started before October 1995 receive, after two months' unemployment or sickness, 50 per cent of mortgage payments for the next four months, but most new borrowers get no help for the first nine months after losing work.

The Child Support Agency

Launched in April 1993, this agency set out to provide a "fair and effective service for the assessment and payment of maintenance... [and] help parents with care of children to make informed choices about whether to take up employment." The intention is of course to thereby reduce the reliance of one-parent families on state benefits.

There are now nearly one and a half million lone parents in Britain and this number is growing by over 100,000 a year. About three quarters of them receive state benefits, which the DSS currently estimates amounts to be around £9 billion a year.

The Agency's first two years were punctuated by headline stories about numerous unfair judgements, causing much suffering and several suicides. A major review of its methods was carried out in December 1994, following the replacement of its first Director. This resulted in the shelving of all cases where Income Support has been paid since before April 1993 in order to concentrate on new cases, where there is less chance of causing trouble.

With a budget for 1996-97 of £213 million, the Agency has a target to collect or arrange payment of at least £380 million of maintenance. Other targets focus on improving the efficiency and accuracy of assessment. Previously, targets have included specific benefit savings. In 1994-95 the target was exceeded, with an estimated £480 million saved.

Child Benefit

There has been much debate over whether the cost of this universal benefit can now be justified. Rich and poor alike receive £10.80 a week for their first child and £8.80 for subsequent children, payable until they leave full-time education. Critics argue that it should be means-tested but the votes of the seven million families who currently receive it probably represent a politically insurmountable obstacle to reform. It continues to be increased each year in line with inflation.

Housing Benefit

This is provided as rent rebates to local authority tenants, and rent allowance paid to people renting from private landlords and housing associations. About five million people have part or all their rent paid by the benefit.

117

Rent allowances amount to £5.7 billion and have recently been the fastest rising element of social security. They have trebled in the last six years but the government is now trying to limit the annual increase to 7 per cent. To help achieve this by encouraging people to find cheaper accommodation, Housing Benefit will now only fully meet rents up to local reference levels. Only 50 per cent of the rent above this level will be paid to most claimants, but none at all for single under-25s with no children.

Rent rebate costs £5.8 billion, and this too has been rising rapidly, largely because of the government policy of making local authorities raise rents nearer to market levels. This policy has now been reversed and authorities are being encouraged to freeze rent levels, in real terms, until 1999.

In England and Wales rent rebate is not actually a rebate to tenants, but the rent foregone by each local authority in respect of tenants who are eligible for the benefit. The cost to the authority is repaid in full by the DoE and the Welsh Office through the rent rebate subsidy, unless this would produce a surplus on its overall Housing Revenue Account, see Chapter 8.

The Cost of Fraud

The government estimates that social security fraud, largely by individuals and gangs making multiple claims, costs well over £2 billion. For Income Support the level is estimated at over £400 million but Housing Benefit fraud is the main problem. Officially it is estimated at about £1 billion but unofficial estimates are as high as £2 billion.

The fraud teams of the Benefits Agency and Employment Service have recently been merged to create the Benefit Fraud Investigation Service. This investigates fraud by individuals while the Benefits's Agency's Organised Fraud Investigation teams deal with the work of professional criminals. The two units together cost about £100 million a year but in 1994-95, the latest year for which data are available, about £720 million worth of fraudulent claims were stopped, across all benefits administered by the Agency.

Greater attention is now being given to combatting Housing Benefit fraud. Local authorities have statutory responsibility for its investigation but, with reimbursement of the benefit from central government, have in the past not had a great incentive to spend money trying to reduce fraudulent claims. In 1994-95 they saved only £170 million but are set to improve substantially on this following a mixture of incentives and penalties from central government.

The Cost of Fraud

Other Benefits

	'000s people	£ billion
Family Credit	700	1.9
One-Parent Benefit	1,100	0.3
Maternity Pay and Allowance	12	0.5
Widows Benefit	290	1.1
Social Fund	n/a	0.2
Industrial Injuries Disablement Benefit	250	0.7
Industrial Death Benefit	20	0.1

Family Credit is an "in-work" benefit designed to encourage low-income couples and lone parents into work by bridging the poverty trap, encountered on moving from Income Support to part-time work of 16 hours a week or more, or low-paid full-time work. Six-month awards are made on the basis of the level of income and child care charges.

Because the government believes that the benefits system has given preferential treatment in recent years to single parents as opposed to couples with children, the one-parent benefit was frozen in the 1995 budget, together with the lone-parent income support premium, at £6.30 and £5.20 respectively. The saving, compared with increasing the benefits in line with inflation, is about £15 million.

The Social Fund is expected to pay out about £80 million on automatic cold weather payments of £8.50 to recipients of Income Support, but most of its spending is in the form of discretionary loans, which return to the Fund on repayment. So although the new money for loans is only £143 million, the total money available, including recycled loans, is about £400 million.

Administration

The Department of Social Security administers most benefits for England, Scotland and Wales, through the Benefits Agency, but local authorities administer Housing Benefit and Council Tax Benefit and the Employment Service administers the Job Seeker's Allowance.

Benefit Administration
1996-97: £4,250 million

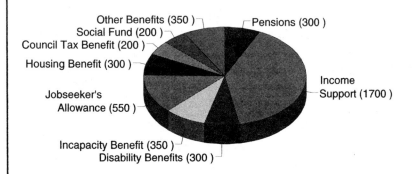

Other Benefits (350)
Social Fund (200)
Council Tax Benefit (200)
Housing Benefit (300)
Jobseeker's Allowance (550)
Incapacity Benefit (350)
Disability Benefits (300)
Pensions (300)
Income Support (1700)

Although relatively small in comparison with other administration costs, the cost of administering the Social Fund is very nearly as much as its net budget because of the necessity of case by case assessment and the administering of loan recovery.

Another £250 million of administration and miscellaneous services does not relate to specific benefits.

Further Information

Social Security Annual Report, The Government's Expenditure Plans 1996-97 to 1998-89. Cm 3213, HMSO.

Spending in this sector is dominated by EC policies and schemes. Some of these get additional funding from MAFF and the agricultural departments of the Welsh, Scottish and Northern Ireland Offices, while other agricultural programmes are purely UK-funded. For this and the next few years, the costs resulting from BSE will be a major item. The following chart shows total spending, including that by local authorities.

Agriculture, Food etc. 1996-97: £5,521 million

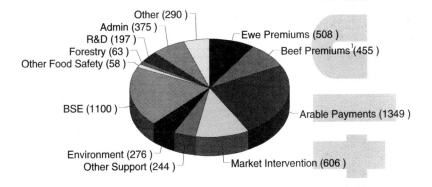

Other (290)
Admin (375)
R&D (197)
Forestry (63)
Other Food Safety (58)
BSE (1100)
Environment (276)
Other Support (244)

Ewe Premiums (508)
Beef Premiums[1] (455)
Arable Payments (1349)
Market Intervention (606)

1 Beef Premium BSE supplement is included under 'BSE'.

£3.4 billion of the £5.5 billion total is paid for by the EC's European Agricultural Guidance and Guarantee Fund (EAGGF). As this money comes out of what we pay the EC, and agree on jointly, it is regarded as government spending. (For gross and net payments to the Community see Chapter 16.)

Livestock Premiums

The Ewe and Beef Premium schemes make payments to farmers, partly within quota limits, according to the number of these animals that they have. Ewes earn around £20 a head. For beef, the pie chart shows the expenditure expected to result from the rates of £93 for each male beef animal and £124 for cows suckling beef calves, agreed before the BSE crisis. The effect of the latter is discussed below.

Arable Area Payments

This scheme only began in 1993 and is the main cause of the 50 per cent increase (before the effect of BSE) in the government's total spending on agriculture over the last four years. Farmers receive fixed payments per hectare of different crops, and for setting aside land from production. The amounts spent on each are as follows:

	£ million
Cereals	764
Oilseeds	275
Protein (e.g. beans)	87
Set-aside	223

Market Intervention

This involves the purchase of products at a minimum price to guarantee a market, and the payment of export refunds to producers to make up the difference between the world price they receive and the agreed minimum price. The first of these is the mechanism notorious for creating Europe's food mountains. In theory the produce could be sold off when the market price rose above the minimum, but often it did not. This resulted in massive surpluses that were either given away as food aid or sold cheaply ("dumped") outside the

Community, often with severe consequences for small overseas producers. Changes to these schemes, and current high commodity prices, mean that EC intervention stocks are now quite small, but it is recognised that stocks will build up again if commodity prices fall.

A number of such intervention schemes apply to the UK, administered by the Intervention Board rather than the agriculture departments. The largest ones are:

	£ million
Milk and milk products	201
Cereals	89
Sugar	135
Beef and veal	78

The Common Agricultural Policy and its Reform

CAP spending is decided by the EC, and this year in the UK comes to around £3.4 billion. The bulk of this is for the Livestock Premium, Arable Payments and Market Intervention schemes though contributions to BSE measures are now also significant. The CAP developed out of the shortages of World War II, and reflects Europe's aim for a degree of self-sufficiency in food, and for support to its rural communities. (The UK is now about 60 per cent self-sufficient in all food and animal feed, and about 75 per cent self-sufficient in indigenous crops.)

Britain has always pressed for reform to reduce the cost of the CAP, and to introduce a more free market in agricultural products. Several such reforms have taken place: milk, milk product and meat support prices are being reduced in real terms, but to varying degrees.

The greatest change in market support has been the reduction in the price for cereals, but the direct acreage payments are more than compensating for this, and high world prices are making intervention buying less necessary. The change in the method of supporting arable farmers should however lead to less intensive production in the longer term, as high yields are no longer guaranteed to be well rewarded.

Other changes have included the wider use of quotas to limit production, and limiting the volumes of subsidised exports. Even so, it is generally felt that the CAP is unsustainable without radical reform.

Other Support

This category covers a large number of relatively small programmes aimed at 'improving the economic performance of the agriculture, fishing and food industries' and is funded by the agriculture departments alone, i.e. with no EC involvement. The largest of these programmes are for MAFF expenditure on:

£ million

Fisheries	39
Plant and Animal Diseases[1]	39
Rural Economy	19
Royal Botanical Gardens	19

1 Additional to spending on Food Safety, below.

The grant to Kew Gardens meets about three-quarters of its costs, including botanical research and the maintenance of unique collections of living and preserved plants.

Including Scottish Office funding, total support for fisheries is about £60 million.

Protecting the Environment

The number of schemes specifically designed to encourage good environmental stewardship has grown in recent years. The government meets most of their costs but there is some support from the EAGGF.

The largest environmental scheme is the longstanding Hill Livestock Compensatory Allowances (£110 million) paid on breeding cows and ewes in upland areas, in order to help maintain the viability of traditional and environmentally sympathetic production systems. Farmers in severely disadvantaged areas receive the HLCA at a rates of £48 per cow and up to £6 per ewe; in other disadvantaged areas the rates are half these. The scheme has been cut by about £50 million since 1992, but this is more than balanced by increases in the livestock premiums.

Farmers and landowners within Environmentally Sensitive Areas are paid £56 million for carrying out agreed management plans, while another £27 million of farm grants is provided for conservation-based improvement plans on other land. A third "countryside stewardship" scheme costs nearly £20 million and then there are several smaller schemes relating to different habitats.

Bovine Spongiform Encephalopathy (BSE)

Prior to 1996-97, total government spending on measures against BSE had been £184 million (excluding research). Most of this took the form of compensation payments to farmers whose cattle showed signs of the disease, and the costs of slaughter and disposal of carcases. The original plans for 1996-97 envisaged a corresponding spend of £16 million. But the ban on the export of British beef (see Box) forced the introduction of much more substantial measures, whose total cost over the next few years is likely to exceed £2.5 billion.

The estimated cost of BSE measures in 1996-97 is now in the region of £1.1 billion, though this figure (as of July 1996) is still a little uncertain: some programme details are not fully agreed, and rates of implementation not fully known. It is estimated that roughly £500 million of the total will be needed to remove from the food chain, at the end of their useful lives, all cattle older than 30 months. The selective cull of animals born in the same groups as those found to have BSE will cost a further £100 million or so. For these two measures, the EC pays 70 per cent of the purchase cost of the animals, and so contributes around £215 million.

To compensate farmers across Europe as a whole for the slump in the beef market, the EC has increased the Special Beef and Suckler Cow premiums by £20 and £23 per animal respectively, above the levels previously decided (and given in the section above on Livestock Premiums). This will cost about £85 million in the UK. The EC has also made available sums to members states according to their total cattle numbers. Britain's share of this is some £27 million, to be used to make discretionary payments on a basis still to be decided. Other EC-supported programmes likely to be impacted by BSE are the calf processing scheme and beef intervention payments.

The total EC help for Britain overall, in 1996-97, is estimated at £390 million. But these additional receipts substantially affect the abatement of our contribution to the EC budget (explained in Chapter 16), so the net effect of this help is only about £134 million.

Costs to be borne by the government alone, with no EC help, include support to renderers of £118 million, to abattoirs of £130 million, and additional inspection and enforcement costs of £57 million.

BSE: A Short History

Fist noticed in April 1985, the disease was confirmed in September 1986. Its origin is uncertain, but is thought to have come from the use of meat-and-bone meal in animal feed - a practice that has been commercial for some decades - combined with more recent changes in the processes used at rendering plants. By the time the ban on feeding ruminant protein to ruminants was introduced in mid-1988, cases of BSE had risen to 200 a month, and in late 1989 the ban on using specified bovine offal in human food was introduced. BSE cases continued to rise, peaking in 1992 at 3000 a month - equivalent, on an annual basis, to one in 300 of all UK cattle becoming infected. These levels, plus the occurrence of BSE in cattle born after the feed ban date, triggered more rigorous inspections at meat processing sites. These found very significant failings, and led in 1995 to new measures including offal staining. Both before and after this period the government, on the basis of actions taken so far, was denying any possible human health risk, and the EC had been permitting the export of young cattle. However, in March 1996 (with new cases still at around 1000 a month) the possible link between BSE and Creutzfeldt-Jakob Disease (CJD) was officially announced, and the world-wide export ban on British beef followed. It took until the Florence summit in June 1996 before measures necessary for the ban to be lifted were agreed, but with no specific timetable being set.

BSE: A Short History

Other Food Safety

The largest spend on food safety is £24 million for the control and eradication of the cattle diseases Brucellosis and Tuberculosis, with a further £34 million covering spending on the safe use of pesticides, salmonella control, and hygiene inspections.

Forestry

The Forestry Commission owns and manages about 40 per cent of Britain's woodland - some 863,000 hectares - and 220,000 hectares of other land. Its income and expenditure are as follows:

Income		Expenditure	
Timber Sales	144	Forest Enterprise costs	187
Property Sales	20	Private woodland grants	40
MAFF grant	63		
		Total	227
Total	227		

The government grant can thus be regarded as providing a subsidy of £23 million to the Forest Enterprise, the public forestry operation, and meeting the full cost of the £40 million grants to private landowners under schemes operated by the Forest Authority. Most of these grants are for new planting, but £5 million is for replanting and £10 million for the management of existing woodland.

The £20 million in property sales is an on-going activity. Since 1981 about £230 million has been raised from the sale of some 220,000 hectares of land, i.e. about 20 per cent of current holdings.

Research and Development

Spending on R&D covers a wide range of programmes, of which the largest are horticultural and food safety research, at about £11 million each.

Support & Administration

As well as the central costs of MAFF and the other agricultural departments, this includes the administration costs of the Intervention Board, and the costs of central services such as property management, personnel, and computers. ADAS, the government Veterinary Services, and some other services are now Executive Agencies, and have become almost entirely self-supporting.

Further Information

Ministry of Agriculture, Fisheries and Food and the Intervention Board, Departmental Report 1996. Cm 3204, HMSO.

Serving Scotland's Needs. Departments of the Secretary of State for Scotland, and the Forestry Commission Annual Report, 1996. Cm 3214, HMSO.

Agriculture in the UK, Annual, HMSO.

Heritage and leisure stand in contrast to the utilitarian principle that underlies most government spending. We find here the provision of facilities for many forms of enjoyment, for us and for generations to come, that can only be provided collectively and would not be viable commercially.

But alongside this there is the hard-nosed sponsorship of the tourism, media and arts industries - more akin to the role of the DTI.

Heritage and Leisure
1996-97: £2,860 million

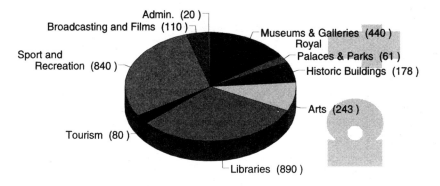

Admin. (20)
Broadcasting and Films (110)
Sport and Recreation (840)
Tourism (80)
Museums & Galleries (440)
Royal Palaces & Parks (61)
Historic Buildings (178)
Arts (243)
Libraries (890)

The Department of National Heritage (DNH) looks after central government's involvement in this area, mainly supporting museums, galleries, historic buildings and the arts, with a budget of about £1 billion. Local authorities' spending, particularly on sport and libraries, adds a further £1.6 billion, with the Scottish, Welsh and Northern Ireland Offices accounting for the rest.

Museums and Galleries

Most of the 2,000+ museums and galleries in Britain are publicly owned and many of the rest receive local authority support. Those funded by the DNH are as follows:

National Museums and Galleries
DNH Support, 1996-97: £213m

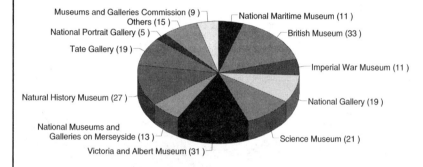

Museums and Galleries Commission (9)
Others (15)
National Portrait Gallery (5)
Tate Gallery (19)
Natural History Museum (27)
National Museums and Galleries on Merseyside (13)
Victoria and Albert Museum (31)
National Maritime Museum (11)
British Museum (33)
Imperial War Museum (11)
National Gallery (19)
Science Museum (21)

When most national museums introduced charges in the late 1980s attendances fell, unsurprisingly, so the government subsidy per visitor ironically rose. Attendance then steadily increased by about 20 per cent between 1989-90 and 1994-95 but then fell back slightly in 1995-96. Based on expected visits during 1996-97, the subsidies per visitor are now as follows:

Subsidies per Visitor, 1996-97

National Maritime Museum	£26.30
Victoria and Albert Museum	£17.00
Natural History Museum	£16.10
National Museums and Galleries on Merseyside	£10.20
Imperial War Museum	£8.60
Science Museum	£8.20
Tate Gallery	£7.80
National Portrait Gallery	£6.10
British Museum	£5.40
National Gallery	£4.30

This does not, of course, tell the whole cost-benefit story - the value of preserving exhibits and collections for posterity cannot be quantified.

The Museums and Galleries Commission provides advice and support, largely to local government, and through them is trying to build up a picture of conservation and collection care at the 1,600 museums on its register.

Spending by local authorities, operating their own museums and providing grants to others, is about £180 million.

Royal Palaces and Parks

The Royal Household Property Service receives a grant of £21 million for maintenance of the fabric of the occupied Royal Palaces. The cost to the state of the restoration of Windsor Castle following the 1993 fire will be about £10 million over five years, another £25 million coming from visitor receipts from Buckingham Palace and the Castle itself.

The five unoccupied palaces - Hampton Court Palace, Kensington Palace's public State Apartments (with the Royal Ceremonial Dress Collection and Orangery), the Tower of London, Kew Palace with Queen Charlotte's Cottage and the Banqueting House in Whitehall - are preserved and run by the Historic Royal Palaces Agency. Government support is up sharply in 1996-97, from £5 million to £13 million, because of a £6 million increase in capital spending combined with lower receipts. In addition to maintaining its own buildings, the Agency is also contributing £6 million this year (as well as last) to the creation of the new Royal Armouries museum in Leeds, which will take some of the collection from the Tower of London.

Without the benefit of an income from visitors, the royal parks require more government funds than the palaces to maintain. The Royal Parks Agency receives £23 million to offer "...peaceful enjoyment, recreation, entertainment and delight".

Also included in this segment of the pie chart is a further £4 million spent by the DNH on public buildings and ceremonial functions.

Historic Buildings

Although English Heritage, Historic Scotland and Cadw receive some income from admission charges and membership subscriptions, their government grants of £105, £32 and £11 million respectively account for about 85 per cent of their income. They spend about a fifth of this maintaining their own properties, give away more than a third in grants to other organisations, especially the National Trust, and spend most of the rest on research and providing advice.

While these organisations maintain buildings, the National Heritage Memorial Fund (NHMF) buys more of them - and other important heritage - for the nation, to prevent them being lost. Its £9-12 million a year has in the past been topped-up from the government's contingency reserve when necessary, e.g. to save Weston Park in Shropshire, but it is now also responsible for distributing the new National Heritage Memorial Fund - around £300 million in 1996-97, taking it into a new league. Government funding has fallen slightly, to £8 million. Any further cut would clearly compromise the government's declaration that Lottery funding will not replace government funding, but in this case such a move would not seem unreasonable, so great has been the increase in resources.

Another £11 million allows the Royal Commission on the Historical Monuments of England to maintain records, including old photographs, of historic sites and monuments. In 1994 it moved to the former Great Western Railway's General Office in Swindon, to set up the National Monuments Record Centre. There is a similar Commission for Scottish monuments, which receives £3 million from the Scottish Office.

The National Lottery

Apart from the £2 million to fund the Office of the National Lottery (OFLOT), Lottery proceeds are outside our definition of government spending (see Chapter 1) and so are not included in the pie chart above. But we cannot ignore them, as they do fall within the government's broader definition of public spending, and equal about 55 per cent of all other government spending on heritage and leisure.

Setting up the National Lottery, aiming to "improve the quality of life for everyone in the UK and leave a lasting legacy for future generations", was one of the main objectives for the DNH when it was created in 1992. The lottery has been a greater success (in its own terms) than expected, with an average spend of around £3 per week by each of its 30 million or so participants. In 1995-96 this created a turnover of £5.2 billion, about a two-thirds of which came from the weekly draw, with most of the rest from scratchcards.

Sales from the on-line game have held pretty steady at £60-70 million per week for most weeks, with a peak (in a roll-over week) of £128 million. For the Instants game, sales grew rapidly to £40 million a week but have since declined steadily, and are currently at less than half this figure.

Estimated income for this year, and its allocation, are as follows:

Allocation of Lottery Income
1996-97 Estimates: £5,600 million

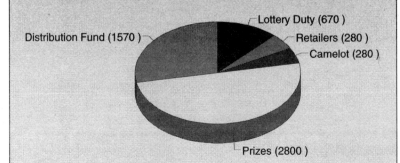

- Lottery Duty (670)
- Distribution Fund (1570)
- Retailers (280)
- Camelot (280)
- Prizes (2800)

(continued overleaf)

The National Lottery

The National Lottery (continued)

In 1995-96, £2.6 billion went as prizes and £1.4 billion to good causes. Camelot Group's £55 million profits attracted criticism although only equal to 4 per cent of the money given to good causes.

After covering OFLOT's costs, the money paid into the Distribution Fund is split equally between the Arts Councils (as a group), Sports Councils (also as a group), the Charities Board, the National Heritage Memorial Fund, and the Millennium Commission. The £1.6 billion expected for 1996-97 will thus give each of the five over £300 million. The funds were initially available for capital projects only, but from 1996-97 can cover some current expenditure.

About 5,000 awards are made each year, most of them of less than £100,000 but the larger grants have included:

The Arts Councils:
> £55 million to Covent Garden
> £30 million to Sadler's Wells
> £12 million to the Globe Theatre

The Sports Councils:
> £100 million to set up a national Academy of Sport to help ensure that all children and young people have access to good sports facilities

The National Heritage Memorial Fund:
> £13 million to buy Sir Winston Churchill's papers
> £10 million for the National Trust in Scotland

The Millennium Commission:
> £50 million for the Millennium Earth Centre for sustainable development, in South Yorkshire
> £50 million for the Tate Gallery
> £42 million for a national cycle network

To date, the Charities Board has tended to make a large number of small grants.

The Arts

Spending on the living arts is dominated by the grants of £186 million, £24 million, £14 million and £7 million to the Arts Councils of England, Scotland,

Wales and Northern Ireland respectively. Local authorities provide support of a further £40 million. Taken together these provide nearly half of the income of the major beneficiaries, or an average subsidy of about £15.60 per attendance.

Nearly a third of the English Art Council's spending is distributed to regional arts boards, while it gives directly £43 million to music, £27 million to drama and £23 million to dance.

Lord Gowrie, chairman of the Arts Council of England, is trying to counter public concern that Council members are not publicly accountable and decide how the money is spent according to their own, rather than popular, taste. Professional excellence is fostered, it is claimed, rather than art "by the people, for the people".

A £3 million grant to the Crafts Council encourages the production and public appreciation of contemporary crafts.

Libraries

Local authorities provide about 5,000 public libraries at a cost of about £800 million. They are well used - the average citizen borrows ten books a year.

The British Library's operating costs in 1996-97 are £112 million, of which £80 million is government support from the DNH. Another £22 million is being spent finishing off its new building in St Pancras, which will have cost about £500 million by the time it is completed in 1997.

The government makes payments to authors whose books are borrowed from libraries, through the Public Lending Right. This totals about £5 million a year.

Tourism

Tourism is a serious business. It contributes about £35 billion to the GDP - about 5 per cent of the total - and about a third of which comes from some 25 million overseas visitors. To maintain and improve on these figures the Department provides £36 million to the British Tourist Authority to promote Britain abroad, and £10 million to the English Tourist Board to promote tourism at home and to encourage expansion and improved standards within the industry. Scotland, Wales and Northern Ireland have their own Tourist Boards which each receive around £15 million.

The Department itself works with other parts of government to remove potential hindrances to tourism that have been identified by the industry, such as certain food hygiene and fire safety regulations.

Broadcasting and Films

Of the £85 million spent on broadcasting, £73 million supports the Welsh fourth channel, Sianel Pedwar Cymru (S4C). The government took over its funding in January 1993 from the ITV companies. Another £10 million is the grant to Gaelic Broadcasting, while £2 million funds the Broadcasting Standards Council and the Broadcasting Complaints Commission.

The British Film Institute receives £17 million a year - about half of its total income - from the government. Some it passes on to regional arts bodies but most of it goes into its own operations, which include the National Film Theatre, the National Film and Television Archive and the Museum of the Moving Image.

Another £7 million spending goes to the following bodies:

National Film and TV School	£1.9m
British Screen Finance Ltd	£2.0m
European Co-production Fund Ltd	£2.0m
British Film Commission	£0.8m

The BBC

The full costs of the BBC's "home" broadcasting, i.e. to the UK, are met from the television licence fee. The estimated 1996-97 income is £1,932 million, of which £2 million is retained by the DNH to cover broadcasting-related costs and the rest is passed on to the BBC. But as a public corporation rather than part of government, its revenue-financed spending is excluded from true government spending.

As overseas listeners pay no license fee, the costs of the BBC's World Service are met by the Foreign Office, see Chapter 3.

The BBC

Sport and Recreation

Local authorities spend about £900 million on sports facilities, including swimming pools and leisure centres, while central government supports the Sports Councils to the tune of £47 million for the UK and England Councils together, £9 million for Scotland, £7 million for Wales and £3 million for Northern Ireland. The government contributes a further £3 million of co-funding through the business sponsorship incentive scheme, Sportsmatch.

The four Sports Councils for England, Scotland, Wales and Northern Ireland are responsible for distribution of National Lottery money and focus especially on young people, while the new UK Sports Council will have general national responsibilities for sport defined as follows:

- leading the campaign against the misuse of drugs through education and dope tests

- providing expert sports coaching through its National Coaching Foundation

- providing scientific and medical support and advice to individual sports' governing bodies

Further Information

Department of National Heritage Annual Report. The Government's Expenditure Plans, 1996-97 to 1998-99. Cm 3211, HMSO.

Tourism: Competing with the Best. Department of National Heritage, 1995.

Total spending by local authorities in 1996-97 is estimated at £74.6 billion but most of it is on major services, particularly education and social services, covered in other chapters. This chapter deals with the remaining £5.4 billion, together with finance for the Scottish Water Authorities.

Other Local Services
1996-97: £5,770 million

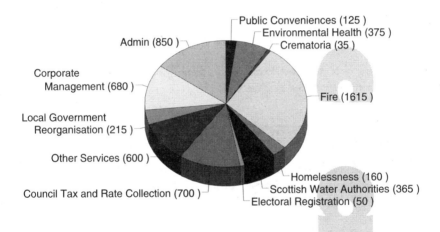

Admin (850)
Public Conveniences (125)
Environmental Health (375)
Crematoria (35)
Corporate Management (680)
Local Government Reorganisation (215)
Fire (1615)
Other Services (600)
Council Tax and Rate Collection (700)
Homelessness (160)
Scottish Water Authorities (365)
Electoral Registration (50)

"Other Services" includes civil defence, a high profile activity during the Cold War but now costing only £20 million. Local authorities are still required by law to maintain up to date plans for civil defence, but following the ending of the perceived threat of nuclear attack a review in 1991 decided to refocus on peacetime disaster planning. Many activities were ended and the decision taken to dispose of the seventeen Regional Government HQs built in the 1950s. The ten already sold have realised only £1.2 million; the last seven will be sold during 1996.

Environmental Health

This covers a wide range of inspection activities, mainly carried out by Environmental Health Officers (EHOs) and their assistants. If costs are allocated between these simply in relation to the time spent on each type of work, the most costly are:

Housing standards	£80 million
Food safety	£65 million
Noise	£36 million
Pollution	£34 million

Other problems dealt with include drainage, pest control, and accumulations of rubbish that represent a health hazard. Meat inspections, of abattoirs and meat in transit, usually cost about £30 million with the costs fully recovered from the inspected companies, but increased inspections for the enforcement of new anti-BSE measures may change this in 1996-97.

EHOs also carry out Health and Safety inspections, costing about £35 million and included in Chapter 5.

Crematoria and Cemeteries

While some people are still buried in churchyards, and there are some private cemetery companies, most provision for the dead is in the hands of local authorities.

Their crematoria carry out about 390,000 cremations a year, and do so in an increasingly business-like manner. Between 1989-90 and 1993-94, while average costs increased by only 20 per cent, to £116 per cremation, charges were raised by over 50 per cent leading to an average profit of £37.

Local authority cemeteries, on the other hand, with charges varying from £35 to £825, were covering less than half of their 1993-94 £80 million costs, relating to about 120,000 burials. So our £35 million estimate for 1996-97 represents about £50 million for the net cost of burials less the crematoria's £15 million surplus.

The Fire Service

Fires kill around 700 people each year in Britain, and cause about £600 million worth of damage to insured property. (Information is only available through insurance claims, so other damage cannot be costed.) As well as trying to reduce these figures, the fire service also deals with other emergencies and rescues, particularly involving road accidents.

60,000 firefighters are employed, who respond to over a million calls each year. Many are false alarms but about 450,000 fires are attended and 170,000 non-fire emergencies. Roughly 40 per cent of the fires involve casualties or damage to property, and some 4,000 people a year are rescued.

Homelessness

Of the roughly 300,000 individuals and households that claim homelessness each year, 35-40 per cent are accepted by the local authority and found some sort of accommodation. In 1993-94, the latest year for which data are available, about one quarter (some 30,000) were given local authority tenancies and 10,000 referred to Housing Associations. Estimates of the temporary accommodation provided for the majority, obtained by extrapolating from England and Wales data, are as follows:

Accommodation for the Homeless

Type of accommodation	Individuals/Households	Net Cost[1]
Hostels	26,000	£20m
Bed and Breakfast	25,000	£23m
Leasehold properties	13,000	£59m
Women's refuges	3,500	n/a
Other	16,000	n/a

1 After charges to clients, and housing benefit.

Other costs cover administration and client welfare.

Scottish Water Authorities

In April 1996, three water authorities were created in Scotland as public corporations, to take over responsibility for water and sewerage from local authorities. Capital spending is partly financed by £275 million of borrowing this year. If, as we expect, this is borrowed from central government rather than the market, then it is included within our definition of government spending. The other £90 million is a straight central government subsidy of operating costs, to keep down the charges to customers.

Council Tax and Business Rate Collection

It costs local authorities about £400 million to collect the Council Tax and £100 million to collect the rates levied on local businesses, but £87 million of the latter is netted off the income (at 0.6 per cent) and so not counted as spending. The DoE, Scottish and Welsh Offices reimburse the costs of the valuations on which the taxes and rates are based, carried out by the Valuation Office Agency and the Valuation Tribunals.

There are 112 local Valuation Offices in England, and 56 Valuation Tribunals that deal with appeals involving disputed valuations. For 1996-97 their workloads and costs are forecast to be as follows:

Valuation Work in England

	Cases	Unit cost	Total Cost
Valuation Offices			
Non-domestic ratings	538,000	£190	£102m
Council Tax banding	482,000	£41	£20m
Valuation Tribunals			
Non-domestic ratings	305,000	£29	£9m
Council Tax banding	90,000	£29	£2m

We also include in the £700 million shown on the pie chart an estimate of £70 million for the collection of arrears, especially of poll tax, dating back to 1992-93 and earlier. (English authorities budgeted £95 million for this in 1995-96.)

Local Government Reorganisation

Local government in Wales and Scotland was reduced to a single tier in April 1996. Scotland's nine regional and 53 District councils have been replaced by 29 unitary authorities, while the eight counties and 37 Districts in Wales have given way to 22 authorities. The Scottish and Welsh Offices are providing the new authorities with an additional £66 million and £40 million respectively, in 1996-97, to help meet the costs of the transition.

Changes in England, following the Local Government Commission's reviews of Districts and shire counties, are somewhat more cautious. Structural changes were made to five counties in April 1996 and changes for another 23 are planned. These could lead to up to the creation of around 40 unitary authorities. The cost this year is £109 million, most of which is in the form of borrowing by the new authorities.

Corporate Management and Administration

These look large on the pie chart but represent overheads relating to all local authority services, of which we include only a small proportion in this chapter. Taken together they represent only about 2 per cent of local authority spending.

Further Information

Local Authority Performance Indicators, March 1996, Audit Commission, HMSO

Local Government Financial Statistics No6, 1995. Government Statistical Service, DoE, HMSO.

Home Office Annual Report, 1996. Cm 3208, HMSO.

CIPFA, the professional accounting body for the public sector, publish many annual statistical reports on different areas of local authority spending. Those relating to this chapter are:

Local Government Comparative Statistics

Environmental Health Statistics

Homelessness Statistics

Crematoria Statistics

Cemetery Statistics

Contributions to the European Community

Although we contribute over £7 billion to the EC we get back from Brussels most of this, as different types of grant for various purposes. These receipts have been included with other public spending under the relevant chapters above, but here we discuss the whole picture: our gross contributions, our receipts and our resulting net contribution.

Britain's Payments to the EC

European Community budgets operate on calendar, rather than financial years, so breakdowns of EC income and spending are only available on this basis. Our contribution to the 1996 Budget is built up from several separately assessed components:

UK Payments to the EC Budget, 1996[1]

Agricultural Levies	£0.15bn
Sugar Levies	£0.06bn
Customs duties	£2.09bn
VAT contributions	£4.97bn
GNP-based contributions	£3.15bn
Total	£10.42bn
less UK Abatement - £2.95bn	£7.47bn

1 Before any adjustments to pay for BSE measures.

Agricultural levies are charged on produce imported into the UK from outside the EC, and are designed to offset the difference between world prices and those within the Community.

Sugar levies are charged on the production of EC sugar to help stabilise EC demand; they are partly used to subsidise the export of surplus quota Community sugar onto the World Market.

Customs duties are those on imports to the UK from non-member countries. (On these duties, and on the two levies above, we retain 10 per cent of the revenue to cover the costs of collection.)

VAT is linked in the public mind with payments to the EC, but the £5 billion above represents only about 11 per cent of the total VAT collected by the government.

GNP-based contributions demand the same percentage of each member state's GNP - currently 0.4 per cent.

The **UK Abatement** system was negotiated by Mrs Thatcher at the Fontainbleu Summit in 1984. It reduces our net contributions (i.e. payments less receipts) to about one third of what they would otherwise be.

EC or EU?

Although often used synonymously, the European Community and the European Union are distinct legal entities. The European Community is the new designation of the former European Economic Community (EEC), renamed at the Maastricht treaty and with continuing general responsibility for economic and trade matters. While usually shortened to "EC", this strictly is the abbreviation of the European Communi*ties*, which include also the much smaller European Coal and Steel Community and Euratom.

The EU was created at Maastricht by the addition of two other policy areas in which the member states are pledged to cooperate: a Common Foreign and Security Policy, and Justice and Home Affairs.

EC or EU? (side tab)

The EC Budget, and Contributions of other Member States

The revenue the EC can raise is fixed as a percentage of the overall Community GNP and, since the Community is not allowed to borrow, this also limits expenditure. Although the EC proposes the budget, the Council of Ministers has the final say on 'compulsory' spending (largely the agricultural spending, about half the Community's budget) and the European Parliament on the remainder. The 1996 budget is 79 billion ecus, equivalent to £69.4 billion.

Community spending has grown over time, from about 0.5 per cent of its overall GNP in the 1970s to around 1 per cent in the late 1980s, and is limited this year to 1.2 per cent. It is still planned to rise, but only slowly, with a limit of 1.27 per cent of Community GNP by 1999.

The *UK's* current contribution, after abatement, is only 1 per cent of our GNP. This translates to nearly 11 per cent of the EC's total income, and compares with other countries' contributions as follows:

Contributions to
the EC Budget, 1996

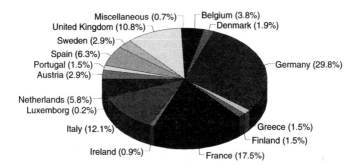

EC Spending

At one time the Common Agricultural Policy totally dominated the spending of the (then) EEC. Efforts to control agricultural spending through various 'Budget Discipline' decisions, as well as the growth of other spending, have reduced it's share - but only to 55 per cent of the budget:

Total EC Spending, 1996
£69.4 billion

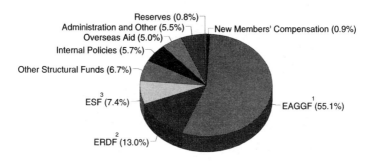

1 European Agricultural Guidance and Guarantee Fund (Does not included the cost of BSE measures, which will add 1.5 - 2.0 per cent.)
2 European Regional Development Fund
3 European Social Fund

The cost to the UK of farming subsidies and other agricultural support programmes is about £3.4 billion this year, or £60 per UK resident. To ensure a further decline in its relative importance, the growth of agricultural support is now limited to a maximum of 74 per cent of the aggregate Community GNP growth rate.

Grants from the ERDF are used for capital works in designated areas, mainly for industrial support, training facilities and roads, while money from the ESF supports training and employment projects in deprived areas. 'Other structural funds' include the £2.1 billion Cohesion Fund, which sponsors environmental and transport infrastructure projects in the poorest members of the community - Greece, Spain, Ireland and Portugal.

Spending on 'Internal Policies' relates mainly to Research and Development and to social and education programmes, while 'Compensation to New Members' represents transitional payments to Austria, Finland and Sweden. The £4.5 billion shown for Overseas Aid is additional to the bilateral (i.e. direct) aid given by member states, see Chapter 3.

EC Payments to the UK

The government tries, of course, to maximise our claim on EC funds. Most agricultural funds are linked directly to agricultural activity and so not amenable to negotiation, but levels of other funding depend upon the strength of the cases put forward by the DTI (overall responsibility), the DfEE (for the ESF) and the DoE (for the ERDF), and are agreed in five-year programmes. Total receipts this year are expected to be £5.2 billion:

UK Receipts from the EC, 1996-97

Agricultural Guidance and Guarantee Fund	£3,390m
Social Fund	£1,068m
Regional Development Fund	£744m
Other	£23m
	———
Total	£5,225m

The government includes the spending of these receipts in its published spending plans (and we have followed this approach). But money from the ERDF has to be seen to be additional to, rather than in place of, normal government spending.

97 per cent of EAGGF receipts are from the 'guarantee' part of the fund and the remainder from the 'guidance' component. The total receipts include £390 million to help pay for the measures to eradicate BSE, see Chapter 13.

The Welsh, Scottish and Northern Ireland Offices administer the ERDF and ESF within their regions, while in England ERDF grants go through the DTI, DoE and the Department for National Heritage, and ESF grants through the DfEE.

Because of its high unemployment and generally greater incidence of deprivation than the rest of the UK, Northern Ireland receives £255 million of the £1.8 billion non-EAGGF receipts. This includes almost 20 per cent of Britain's ERDF funding.

In addition to the official receipts in the table above, a further £0.5 billion or so comes back directly to the private sector, mainly in the form of research funds from the 'Internal Policies' segment of the spending pie-chart.

The UK's Net Contribution to the EC

The original estimates of our net contribution have been affected by EC help for BSE measures, and the effect of this on the UK abatement. On the standard financial year basis on which the receipts above are expressed, the figures are as follows:

- Britain originally expected to contribute, after the abatement, £7.73 billion in 1996-97.

- Our additional BSE receipts mean the abatement is reduced by about £260 million.

- So our contribution to the EC will now be £7.99 billion.

To our £5.22 billion of *receipts*, shown above, we need to add £578 million, which is Britain's share of EC development aid but counted as within our own aid programme, giving £5.80 billion. This leaves the UK government's net contribution to the EC as £2.19 billion.

Taking account of *all* receipts, including those not channelled through the government, the overall net cost to the country of payments to the EC is around £1.7 billion per year, or about £30 a head. To say how this is spent, we can regard it as being split in the same proportions as in the pie-chart's division of the EC's *total* spending, with the exclusion of overseas aid, which we treat as our own in full proportion to our contributions. So nearly £100 million goes to EC administration and most of the rest to agricultural and other support to poorer countries within the EC. In the debate on Europe, this cost must be weighed against the economic benefits of belonging to a large, harmonised market, and wider gains such as political stability.

The other net contributors to the EC are Germany, France, Italy and the Netherlands. In the near future, Austria and Sweden are expected to join this privileged group.

Further Information

Statement on the 1995 Community Budget. Annual, HMSO.

Departmental Report of the Chancellor of the Exchequer's smaller Departments, 1996. Cm 3217, HMSO.

Here we look at the central functions that support the rest of government, through obtaining its finance, setting its budgets, and making certain payments not attributable to particular spending programmes. We also cover the accounting adjustments that complete the full picture of public spending.

Central Management and Finance, 1996-97: £5,440 million

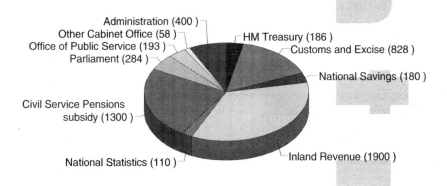

Administration (400)
Other Cabinet Office (58)
Office of Public Service (193)
Parliament (284)
HM Treasury (186)
Customs and Excise (828)
National Savings (180)
Civil Service Pensions subsidy (1300)
National Statistics (110)
Inland Revenue (1900)

+ Debt Interest	**£22,500 million**
+ Accounting Adjustments	**£6,000 million**

H M Treasury

The aim of the Treasury is 'to promote rising prosperity based on sustained economic growth'. Employing 1,000 civil servants, its own administration costs are only £60 million of its total. It spends £25 million a year on coinage, produced by the Royal Mint, and pays £80 million to the Bank of England for banknote production and other services.

It also bears the costs of certain Parliamentary bodies, e.g. the Commonwealth Parliamentary Association, that foster links with elected representative of other countries, and of honours and some state ceremonial expenses. These together come to about £15 million a year.

Paymaster

The Office of HM Paymaster General provides the government's banking services. Its costs of £22 million are met from charges, mainly with respect to its administration of pension payments for the various public sector pension schemes.

Customs and Excise

23,000 staff are employed in the collection of VAT and excise duties on alcohol, tobacco, betting and fuel, as well as the more traditional Customs duties.

In addition to raising revenue a major role now is in combating drug smuggling. In 1994-95 Customs staff seized £500 million worth of illegal drugs and made 2,500 drugs-related arrests. They estimate that by dismantling over two hundred trafficking organisations they prevented another £1200 million worth of drugs from entering the UK market.

Department of National Savings

The Department's main objective is to provide funds that contribute towards meeting the government's borrowing needs. The savings invested by the public totalled £55 billion at March 1996, and grow at £3-4 billion a year. Around 50 million transactions are handled each year.

The pay of the Department's 5,400 staff account for most of its spending, the other significant item being payments to Post Office Counters for acting as its agent.

Inland Revenue

In addition to its own running costs, supporting a staff of some 55,000, the Inland Revenue is responsible for the £250 million paid to non-taxpayers for mortgage interest relief.

Under a ten year programme, tax offices are being replaced by 'new-style' offices of two types - Taxpayer Service Offices carrying out normal tax assessments, and Tax District Offices dealing with technical and compliance work. These are supplemented by mobile enquiry centres and taxpayer surgeries, to achieve increased accessibility despite having fewer offices. About 40 per cent of taxpayers are already served by the new-style offices.

4,000 of the Inland Revenue's staff are in the Valuation Office Agency (VO), which compiles and maintains the council tax and non-domestic rating valuation lists for local authorities. The details of this work, and its costs, are dealt with in Chapter 15. But the VO also carries out some work for the Inland Revenue itself, on Capital Gains Tax and Inheritance Tax assessments, for which it charges the department.

The total shown does not include the £112 million cost of the collection of National Insurance contributions; this is netted off the income.

The Office for National Statistics

This was formed in April 1996 by the merging of the Office of Population Censuses and Surveys with the Central Statistical Office. The new agency now provides a single focus for all government statistics. As well as providing data to government and for business, the Office aims to 'inform the citizen on the state of the nation'. To enhance the service provided in all these areas the comparability, presentation and accessibility of official statistics are to be improved.

The second main function of the ONS is to provide an effective system for the registration of births, marriages and deaths.

The ONS takes over from the OPCS the planning and execution of the ten-yearly census of population and housing, and maintenance of the computerised NHS Central Register of patients. These, and local registrars, provide the data for derivation of national population and health statistics.

The spending figure shown also includes £5 million for the General Register Office for Scotland, which performs similar functions to the old OPCS.

Civil Service Pensions

Departments make their contributions to the Public and Civil Servants Pension Scheme in the same way as other employers fund their pension schemes, but contributions directly pay the pensions of retired members, rather than going into a fund. The departments' payments are included in their staff costs, so we don't count them again here, but they amount to some £1.15 billion.

Together with other income, mainly from employees themselves, total income is about £1.3 billion, in 1996-97. At the same time, over 400,000 ex-civil servants are being paid pensions averaging £4,500. Including also other payments, mainly to dependents, the Scheme is paying out about £3 billion. £400 million of this is paid by the OPS under a special short-term scheme, see below. This leaves a shortfall that we project will be around £1.3 billion, to be paid from the Consolidated Fund.

Parliament

The pay, allowances and pension contributions of members of the House of Commons cost £76 million a year, while the costs of administration, maintenance and capital works are £173 million.

For the Lords the corresponding figures are £7 million for Peers' expenses (they receive no salary) and £34 million for administration etc..

We also include here £6 million covering the cost of the elections for the Northern Ireland Forum, and the running costs of the Forum itself.

Office of Public Service

The OPS is a major part of the Cabinet Office and itself comprises eight executive agencies. These deal with different aspects of the management of the Civil Service and also cross-departmental policies, particularly for de-regulation, which improve the competitiveness of the UK.

The OPS not only *operates* the Principal Civil Service Pension Scheme, but also at present makes a substantial contribution to it. It is paying £400 million in 1996-97 as 80 per cent of the cost of early retirement, redundancy and severance costs incurred under the short-term 'early departure' scheme. This scheme is designed to encourage other government departments and agencies to shed staff, by meeting most of the associated costs.

The reason OPS expenditure is shown at only £193 million is that one of its agencies, the Property Advisers to the Civil Estate (PACE), makes a profit of about £250 million on its management of government buildings.

Other agencies within the OPS are the Recruitment and Assessment Services (RAS), the Central Computer and Telecommunications Agency (CCTA) and the Civil Service College.

The Citizen's Charter Unit is part of the OPS and costs £26 million. It has helped to develop 40 main charters, defining standards of service that the public can expect from the main public services, and thousands of charters for local services such as GPs and police forces.

Other Cabinet Office Spending

Although administratively part of the Cabinet Office, and responsible for about half of its spending, we have included the Security and Intelligence Services in Chapter 2, Defence.

The £59 million shown on the pie chart includes £37 million for the National Audit Office. The NAO audits some 600 accounts of public and international bodies on a commercial basis but also carries out about 50 value for money investigations into the economy, efficiency and effectiveness of public bodies. The identifiable savings resulting from each year's reviews are about £280 million.

The cost of providing about 100 staff and support services for No. 10 Downing Street is around £9 million, and support for the Whips' Office about £2 million. The Parliamentary Council, that is responsible for drafting legislation, costs £4 million.

Debt Interest

The £22.5 billion interest shown on page 151 is net of receipts, and is arrived at as follows:

General Government Debt Interest, 1996-97, £bn

	Payments	Receipts	Net
Central Government	26.8	4.2	22.6
Local Government	0.5	0.6	-0.1
General Government	27.3	4.8	22.5

(These cash payments do not take account of the liability accruing as the result of the increasing value of index-linked gilts, which is included in definitions based on accruals.)

The stock of debt on which these payments are made averages £395 billion over the year, but is expected to have reached £405 billion by March 1997 as a result of new borrowing. The European Union's excessive deficits procedure monitors the ratio between debt and GDP, requiring countries seeking monetary union to keep the ratio below 60 per cent. For the UK, £405 billion represents only 54 per cent of 1996-97's forecast GDP of £751 billion.

In Chapter 18 we show the difference between spending and income, that creates the need for new borrowing.

Administration

This covers £239 million for the DoE and £161 million for the Scottish Office, that cannot be directly attributed to particular programmes.

Accounting Adjustments

There are several of these, of varying degrees of obscurity, but the main ones are VAT payments and depreciation.

Government spending is planned and measured net of VAT refunds, but it is appropriate in reporting total spending to include any VAT paid as real spending, as it represents real income on the other side of the government's balance sheet. So we add it back here - about £3 billion.

Depreciation of assets is also estimated at around £3 billion.

Further Information

The 1996 Report of the Cabinet Office, Privy Council Office and Parliament. Cm 3220, HMSO.

Departmental Report of the Chancellor of the Exchequer's smaller Departments. The Government's Expenditure Plans, 1996-97 to 1998-99. Cm 3217, HMSO.

NAO Annual Report 1996. National Audit Office, July 1996.

Board of the Inland Revenue Report for the year ending 31st March 1995. Cm 3014, HMSO.

The government has a considerable array of instruments for extracting money from the economy to finance public spending. These have been progressively introduced to provide it with enough income to meet its spending plans and borrowing targets and at the same time to allow it to influence economic activity in different ways.

Government Income
1996-97: £279.1 billion

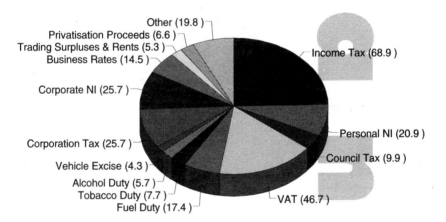

Other (19.8)
Privatisation Proceeds (6.6)
Trading Surpluses & Rents (5.3)
Business Rates (14.5)
Corporate NI (25.7)
Corporation Tax (25.7)
Vehicle Excise (4.3)
Alcohol Duty (5.7)
Tobacco Duty (7.7)
Fuel Duty (17.4)
Income Tax (68.9)
Personal NI (20.9)
Council Tax (9.9)
VAT (46.7)

Consumer spending, industrial investment, the willingness to take on employees and many other important economic drivers can be turned up and down by the choice of where to increase or decrease the burden of taxation. Also, with some taxes having a much higher profile than others, political fortunes can be influenced by the choice.

Definitions

It was noted in Chapter 1 that there are different ways of defining government spending, and that some of the differences relate to whether income is treated as negative spending. The definition of income that we use here has the following conventions, for consistency with our use of GGE(X) as our definition of spending:

- interest and dividend receipts are not included because debt interest payments are expressed net of these;

- only the net income of the National Lottery Distribution Fund is included - the difference between receipts and allocations;

- new money which is owed as a result of the increase in value of index-linked gilts is included as a receipt, to balance the inclusion of this accrued liability under government spending; and

- we treat privatisation proceeds as income. As they represent a loss of assets as well as a cash gain, government accountants do not include them; we do so here because we are primarily interested in the financing of public spending, to which they contribute significantly.

Income Tax

Although this now accounts for only about a quarter of taxation it remains the most conspicuous and painful tax for most people, so there is always great political pressure on the government to reduce it. When the Conservatives came into power in 1979 they wasted no time reducing the basic rate from 33 per cent to 30 per cent. It has now been reduced to 24p in the pound and applies to the £3,900 to £25,500 band of taxable income.

About a quarter of taxpayers have incomes below £3,900 and pay only at the lower 20p rate, while nine per cent pay tax at 40p on their income above £25,500. High earners are a very important source of income: the two million people with incomes above £30,000 pay in total about £28 billion in income tax.

When looking at the scope for cuts in income tax the Chancellor has to bear in mind that it costs the Exchequer about £1.6 billion to cut the basic tax rate by 1 per cent, while raising its starting point by £500 loses nearly £400 million.

National Insurance

Personal and corporate National Insurance (NI) contributions together contribute 15 per cent of general government receipts. Government statistics usually refer to NI as 'social security contributions' but both terms hide the fact that over 12 per cent of this income goes not to pay social security benefits but to the NHS, in place of other taxation income.

Employees earning £61 a week or more pay 2 per cent of the £61, and then 10 per cent of the rest of their earnings up to £455 a week. In addition, their employers pay on a sliding scale up to 10.2 per cent at £210 a week and above. Again, no NI is paid on earnings above the £455 cut-off.

The 10.2 per cent employers' rate will be cut to 10 per cent for 1997-98, the £0.5 billion reduction instead being raised through the virtuous new landfill tax.

Self-employed people pay flat-rate Class 2 contributions at £6.05 a week, plus, on any profits above £6,860, Class 4 national insurance contributions at 6 per cent up to £23,660 - equivalent to the £455 a week limit for employees' NI. Together these contribute about £1.5 billion of the total shown for personal NI contributions in the pie chart.

The £455 (or £23,660 a year) ceiling is in contrast to income tax, where the wealthy pay proportionately more than the poor, and leads to criticism of National Insurance as being a regressive tax. The philosophy behind the different approach is that in an insurance system that pays out standard benefits the rich should not have to pay more than the reasonably well off. Income tax is the chosen instrument for large scale income redistribution (it, rather than NI, funds Income Support for example), and can achieve whatever the government desires in this regard.

Corporation Tax

This is a tax on the profits of companies, public corporations and other profit-making bodies. The full rate of 33 per cent is paid where there is a profit of greater than £1.5 million, but companies with profits of less than £300,000 pay at a rate of 24 per cent, mirroring personal taxation. There is a sliding scale between these upper and lower rates.

Value Added Tax

VAT is paid on most consumer goods with the exceptions of food, children's clothes, transport, books, newspapers and magazines. The standard rate is 17.5 per cent but a reduced rate of 8 per cent is charged on fuel and power for domestic use. The standard rate is lower than that in most other EC countries, although Germany's is only 15 per cent, the EC minimum.

As government spending has increased over the last twenty years much of this growth has been met by increased VAT. The following graph shows how this compares with Income Tax revenue, which has risen only slightly.

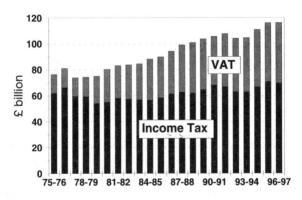

Income Tax and VAT Revenues
(1996-97 prices)

Fuel Duty

The £17 billion comes mainly from petrol and diesel, at a rate of 46 pence per litre for leaded petrol and 40 pence for unleaded and diesel fuel. The rate for super-unleaded was shifted in May 1996 from parity with other unleaded fuel to 44 pence per litre, following concern about the damaging effects of its high benzene content.

The government has a policy of raising the rate by at least five per cent above inflation each year, for environmental reasons, but this also helps to close the gap between Britain and other major EC countries, who tax fuel more heavily.

Vehicle Excise Duty

This is charged at £140 a year for private cars and light goods vehicles. Rates for most heavy goods vehicles have not changed for seven years and are charged between £150 and £4,250, according to their gross weight and the number of axles. For example a 20 tonne (gross weight) truck with three axles pays £990.

Alcohol Duty

Britain's brewers and pub operators blame falling sales on the high level of illegal resale of beer and wine brought across the channel 'for personal consumption'. In the hope of gradually eroding this trade - which reduces government revenues of course, as well as damaging the drinks industry - the duties for beer (24p/pint) and most wine (£1.05/bottle) were not raised with inflation in the 1995 Budget, and that on fortified wine was actually reduced by 12p a bottle. VAT is charged in addition to these duties, of course.

Tobacco Duty

All tobacco products are taxed but by far the greatest revenue comes from cigarettes, which incur £1.79 tax on a packet of twenty (even before VAT adds about another 40 pence). This is one of the highest rates in Europe and has created a substantial tobacco and cigarette smuggling trade. It is the government's policy to increase tobacco taxes by at least three per cent a year in real terms - the 1995 Budget increase was five per cent.

Council Tax

The Council Tax is levied in Great Britain on all dwellings except for student accommodation and some empty properties. (Northern Ireland still uses the old domestic rating system, the income from which is included in 'Other'.) Dwellings are allocated to one of eight bands according to their estimated value, with the Council Tax levied on the highest band being three times that on the lowest. Discounts can be claimed if only one adult lives in the house (25 per cent discount) or the dwelling is not usually occupied (50 per cent), and Council Tax Benefit is available to people on low incomes.

Average Council Tax bills for 1996-97 were up 6.2 per cent on the previous year, three per cent above inflation.

The Funding of Local Authorities

The following pie-chart shows the various sources of money:

Sources of Local Authority Finance
1996-97: £74.6 billion

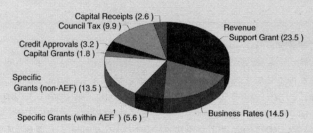

1 Aggregate External Finance

Most money is provided by central government within Aggregate External Finance (AEF), which includes Revenue Support Grant (RSG) and business rates, as well as some specific grants, and totals £43.6 billion. The allocations to each authority are based on central government's judgement of the appropriate levels of current spending on each main service by each authority, known in aggregate as Total Standard Spending, less expected Council Tax receipts.

The specific grants outside AEF are mainly for rent allowances and rebates, council tax rebates and mandatory student awards, all fully funded by central government.

Money for capital spending, expected to be about £8 billion in 1996-97, comes mainly from central government grants, credit approvals (permission to borrow) and a proportion of capital receipts from the sale of council houses and other property and land. Authorities are allowed to use 50 per cent of most capital receipts, but only 25 per cent of receipts from the sale of council houses; the rest of the income has to be used to pay off debt.

While this paints the aggregate picture, the sources of money received by each local authority, and their relative proportions, depend upon their responsibilities. At one extreme, Police authorities in Great Britain receive *half* of their £7.5 billion funding in the form of specific grants within AEF and the rest from RSG, Council Tax and business rates passed on by the local government authorities in their area.

The Funding of Local Authorities

Business Rates

These are rates collected by local authorities from industrial and commercial premises, according to their value. While Scottish local authorities determine the level of their own business rates and retain the income, in England and Wales the levels are set by central government and most of the income is pooled and redistributed. (0.6 per cent, about £90 million, is retained to cover the costs of collection, and not included in the pie chart.)

Privatisation Proceeds

The following graph shows the extent to which government spending has been supported by privatisation proceeds over the last seventeen years, bearing in mind that £5 billion is worth about three per cent on the basic rate of income tax:

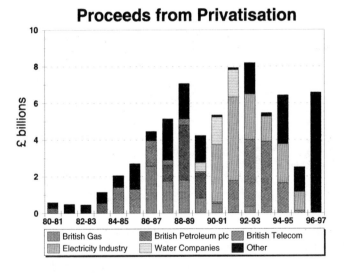

Proceeds from Privatisation

We use a figure of £6.6 billion for 1996-97, rather than the official figure of £4.5 billion, for reasons detailed below. The £4.5 billion is itself an increase from the original plan of £4 billion - an increase made in July 1996 at the same time as the PSBR forecast was increased by £4.5 billion; without it the latter increase would have been £5 billion.

Taking the official privatisation proceeds first, they arise from two major privatisations - Railtrack and British Energy - together with numerous smaller sales. The government receives the first instalment of Railtrack's £1.93 billion proceeds, some £1.2 billion, and £1.4 billion from British Energy's flotation in July. It also gets back its £600 million loans to former Nuclear Electric - £160 million being repaid by British Energy and the other £440 million being sold to private sector lenders. BBC transmitters also are expected to be sold, raising about £100 million. The balance required to meet the Treasury's £4.5 billion target will be made up by the sale of residual equity from earlier privatisations.

(The costs of arranging the privatisations are netted off their gross yield - reducing the direct income from British Energy by £180 million - but most of the money goes to Customs and Excise as stamp duty and VAT.)

The £2.1 billion 'hidden' proceeds that we include are the £645 million from the sale of the housing corporations' loans portfolios and an expected £1.5 billion from the sale of the MoD's 58,000 married quarters.

The government treats the sale of the loans portfolios as negative spending, so this is where our definition of general government spending departs from the government's GGE(X) (see page 3). But the married quarters' sale proceeds do not feature *anywhere* in the government's income and expenditure balance sheet. Despite government claims that important defence contracts could not be signed unless parliament gave the go-ahead for the sale, the MoD budget appears to be fully funded without them. All the MoD will gain will be £100 million for the refurbishment of some properties, while the other £1.4 billion will probably support the government's general expenditure.

Other Income

The residual £20 billion includes many relatively small taxes and duties, of which the largest are:

	£ billion
Customs Duties	2.4
Stamp Duty	2.4
Betting and Gaming Duties	1.7
Inheritance Tax	1.5
Capital Gains Tax	1.0
Petroleum Revenue Tax	1.0
Insurance Premium Tax	0.7
Oil Royalties	0.5
Air Passenger Duty	0.3

Pool Betting Duty is 26.5 per cent of the value of bets placed - reduced from 32.5 per cent in 1995 in response to growing competition from the National Lottery. General Betting Duty, covering horse and greyhound racing for example, was reduced from 7.75 to 6.75 per cent. The Lottery itself contributes about £600 million through the 12 per cent Lottery Duty.

Stamp Duty is charged on certain capital transfers and purchases, with by far the greatest income coming from house purchases. 1 per cent of the price is payable on transactions worth over £30,000.

North Sea oil and gas provide a total income of £3 billion in 1996-97 because, in addition to the Oil Royalties and Petroleum Revenue Tax shown above, £1.5 billion of Corporation Tax results from the production. This income is often seen as a windfall that should be invested for the future.

With sites for the disposal of society's rubbish becoming fewer, and increasing worries about the long-term environmental problems being stored up, the government introduced the Landfill Tax in the 1995 Budget to discourage waste and promote recycling. It comes in to force in October 1996, levying £2 per tonne on inert waste such as rubble and £7 a tonne on all other material, including local authorities' domestic waste. In its first six months it will raise only about £110 million, but around £450 million a year in the future.

Also included here are the £850 million non-fossil fuel levy receipts, the net income of the National Lottery Distribution Fund, and the increased value of index-linked gilts (see Definitions box above).

The General Government Borrowing Requirement (GGBR)

The shortfall between income and spending varies substantially from year to year and, as the difference between two large numbers, is hard to predict. For 1996-97 it is expected to be £28 billion:

Expenditure	£307.1 billion
Income	£279.1 billion
GGBR	£28.0 billion

Borrowing is planned to fall over the next few years so that by 1999-2000 it will be negative, as it was in the late 1980s.

The full Public Sector Borrowing Requirement (PSBR) is actually slightly lower than the GGBR, at £26.9 billion, mainly because nationalised industries are building up deposits, which count as negative borrowing.

The Maastricht terms for qualification for European Monetary Union (EMU) include the 'excessive deficits procedure' which requires nations to have General Government Financial Deficits (GGFDs) of no more than 3 per cent of GDP in 1999. There are several differences in definition between GGFD and the PSBR, the largest of which is that the former does not take privatisation proceeds into account, so it is rather higher. The forecast GGFD for 1996-97 is £30.6 billion, or 4 per cent of GDP, but the government hopes to be down to £6 billion (0.7 per cent of GDP) by 1998-99.

Borrowing to meet the PSBR is carried out mainly by the issue of government stock, usually known as 'gilts' (gilt-edged securities), typically with redemption dates in ten to twenty years. Interest may be paid at a fixed rate or one linked to the RPI. The other significant method of borrowing is National Savings, through which the public lends about £4 billion a year directly to the government.

Because the government spending total does not include the repayment of loans (mainly the principal on maturing gilts), the PSBR is the *net* borrowing required. New borrowing to refinance old loans adds about £4 billion a year to the amount of financing needed.

The PFI and the PSBR

The Private Finance Initiative discussed in Chapter 1 fits well, in the short-term, with the government's concern to bring down the PSBR. But the process of transferring capital spending to the private sector and then buying the service it provides is quite analogous to public borrowing, with future debt servicing being replaced by payments for the use of facilities. The main difference is the length of the lag between the benefits and costs: borrowing money is rapidly followed by interest payments, but through the PFI the government is at present reaping substantial savings without yet incurring any additional costs. So without noting the shift of capital investment to the private sector - about £2 billion in 1996-97, rising to £3 billion a year by 1998-99 - the traditional focus on the PSBR gives a misleading picture of the state of the public finances.

The PFI and the PSBR

Further information

Financial Statement and Budget Report, HM Treasury. November 1995. HMSO.

HM Customs and Excise Annual Report, 1994-1995. Cm 2980, HMSO.

Inland Revenue Statistics, 1995. Central Statistical Office, HMSO.

The charts on the next two pages show general government spending in real terms since 1978-79. The election that brought in the Conservative government was on 3rd May 1979, so the charts start with effectively the last full year of the previous Labour government.

All the charts have been drawn to the same scale so comparisons of relative spending can be made.

The dominance of Social Security spending, and its growth, are clear. The following features also stand out:

- The real-terms decreases over the period, of spending on Defence, Trade & Industry, and Housing.

- The substantial real-terms increases to Law & Order, Education, Health, and Social Services.

- The size, and variability, of Net Debt Interest.

Notes

1. The spending classifications are those used by the Treasury, rather than those we have used in the rest of this book. This is because it would not be practical to repeat our analysis and re-aggregregation for more than one or two earlier years. Most of the categories are very similar, and one or two are the same.

2. The data up to 1995-96 are drawn directly from the recent editions of the Public Expenditure Statistical Analyses (PESA): Cm 2519, 2821 and 3201. We have adjusted them for the effects of inflation to bring them into today's (1996-97) money, using the Treasury's standard GDP deflator.

3. We have generated most of the data for 1996-97 ourselves, based largely on the plans for central government's Control Total provided by PESA. We have added estimates of other (mainly local authority) spending that we have produced in compiling the earlier chapters, to complete the coverage.

General Government Spending in Real Terms (1996-97 prices)

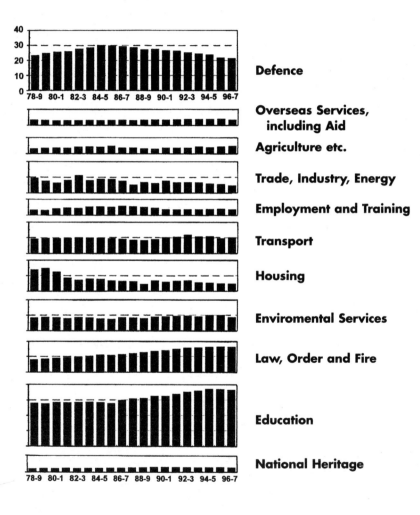

Note: All charts on this and the opposite page are to the same scale.

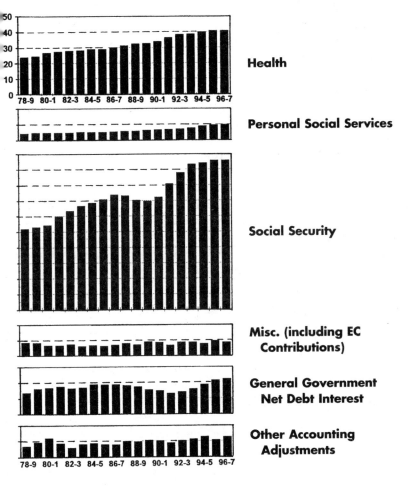

Health

Personal Social Services

Social Security

Misc. (including EC Contributions)

General Government Net Debt Interest

Other Accounting Adjustments

Methodology and Notes

Coverage

Spending on the whole United Kingdom is included. Whitehall Departments vary in their coverage from England alone (e.g. Transport) to the whole of Great Britain (e.g. Social Security), with Northern Ireland having its own versions of all programmes.

While we try in the text to give a fair treatment of the administration of spending programmes throughout the UK, where there are significant differences a bias towards England is inevitable with it accounting for such a dominant share of spending. In many places a laboured explanation of national variations in practice has been sacrificed to readability.

With regard to the level of detail covered, we only have space to itemise and discuss what are *significant* expenditure items within the context of each programme. As the sizes of programmes themselves vary substantially this means that the cut-off level tends to vary, mainly from about £10 million to £100 million. In many instances this means that a lot of good work going on within sub-programmes, schemes and projects costing less than these levels cannot be covered, and we regret this.

Our Main Sources

We cannot cover here in detail the way that we arrived at the estimates of the current year's spending, and of output-related data that we often present alongside them, but we want to outline the main approaches used.

We started from the systematic presentation of government spending provided in the Treasury's *Public Expenditure Statistical Analysis* (PESA), and tried to identify the components of each programme shown there using individual Departments' reports and miscellaneous other sources. This proved very difficult in many cases, until the Treasury provided us with their method of creating the aggregate figures from their spending database, together with the actual costs of the individual components in 1993-94.

This, at present, is the latest year for which their data are 'not liable to any major revisions' but the figures have allowed us to identify estimated outturns or spending plans for the same sub-programmes for later years, usually including 1996-97. The Departmental reports that provide these are usually also the source of the output measures that we quote. We have used the March 1996 editions of PESA and the Departmental reports, and where necessary updated spending estimates using the *Summer Supplementary Estimates*, June 1996.

Estimates of local authority spending were considerably more difficult to obtain than central government spending. Although central government makes estimates of the spending needs of local authorities it cannot publish these as plans. Historical spending for some of their spending areas is published in Departmental reports, but not for the whole of the UK. For much of local authority spending we have had to gross-up and extrapolate - taking account of recent trends - from data for England contained in *Local Authority Financial Statistics*. The latest details provided by the 1996 edition are aggregate local authority budgets for 1995-96. In general we believe we have been able to make reasonable estimates of current spending but where we have serious concerns about the accuracy of the numbers that we present, we make this clear.

Accuracy of the Data

We have dealt above with the methods by which we obtained estimates of spending for 1996-97, based on various data. Here we consider how accurate these data themselves are likely to be.

Some government spending programmes are tightly cash-limited and others can be readily forecast, so the final outturn figures are not likely to be much at variance with those planned. Other data are likely to be less accurate, particularly programmes that are demand-led, such as benefit payments, or some CAP spending, and the year's outcome cannot be so well known in advance. In a few cases, the programmes themselves were not settled at the time of writing this book and, while quite reasonable estimates are possible, the effect of possible programme revisions must be borne in mind; an example being spending on measures related to BSE.

However, we believe that in nearly all cases the degree of uncertainty is not so large as to risk the reader being substantially misled by the figures we present. In most cases we try to indicate the degree of uncertainty by rounding the figures to the level of accuracy we feel the estimates merit, although sometimes, where we directly use numbers that we think others may want to tie back to their sources, we show them faithfully to the nearest £million.

The Re-assignment of Spending between Functional Categories

Readers familiar with PESA will notice that many of our chapters do not correspond neatly with the method of aggregation used therein, although most are very similar. We have chosen to re-assign certain expenditures into categories that we feel are more coherent. For example, we:

- separate employment and training from other industry-related spending;

- include administration of the Job Seeker's Allowance with other social security administration, rather than with the Employment Service;

- include the Security Services with defence spending;

- move the index-linked uplift on certain pensions, that PESA incudes in 'accounting adjustments', into the relevant spending programmes; and

- separate the fire service from spending on law and order.

(In Chapter 19, on Historical Trends, we have reverted to the PESA classifications, as we have not been able to construct spending totals for earlier years consistent with the cost allocations we have used in the rest of the book.)

Handling Small Amounts

Some very small amounts, whose importance would be exaggerated by their separate identification alongside much larger expenditures, have been incorporated into related categories.

Adjusting for Inflation

In all our trend graphs we have adjusted spending for the effects of inflation. We have used the Treasury's 'Adjusted GDP deflator', as published in the PESA and the FSBR, to convert all costs to 1996-97 prices. This adjusts, of course, for the national average level of inflation; in sectors where the mix of products and services involved is quite different there may be slightly different higher or lower inflationary effects, which therefore remain in the series presented.

Key Sources:

Public Expenditure Statistical Analysis 1996-97, HM Treasury, March 1996. Cm 3201, HMSO.

Local Authority Financial Statistics, 1996. CIPFA.

Financial Statement and Budget Report, HM Treasury, November 1995. HMSO.

The precise sums of money voted by parliament to each spending sub-programme are given in:
The Supply Estimates, 1996-97. Main Estimates. HM Treasury, March 1996. HC 261, HMSO.

The Supply Estimates, 1996-97. Summer Supplementary Estimates. HM Treasury, June 1996. HC 427, HMSO

With so much of government now split into Next Steps Agencies the summaries of their activities provided by the following report were frequently useful:
Next Steps Agencies in Government Review, 1995. Cm 3164, HMSO.

Accruals   As an alternative to the simple measurement of cash flows, accruals include also any changes in the money that is owed.

Agencies   Usually used here to refer to 'Next Steps' Agencies - parts of government departments that have well-defined tasks and formal relationships with the rest of the department. See Chapter 1.

Aggregate External Finance   The envelope of external support for local authority services which are also funded from the council tax. It comprises revenue support grant (qv), payments from the yield of business rates (qv), and certain specific grants. See Chapter 18.

Business ('Non-domestic') Rates   The contribution towards the cost of local authority services paid by the occupiers of non-domestic property, principally businesses. The rate bill for a property depends on its rateable value and the poundage for the year in question.

Capital Spending   Capital expenditure on physical assets, expenditure on stocks and grants, and lending for capital purposes.

Central Government   Comprises Parliament, government departments and the Northern Ireland departments, extra-departmental government funds (the largest of which is the National Insurance Fund) and a substantial number of other bodies which are controlled by departments.

CIPFA   The Chartered Institute of Public Finance and Accountancy. The professional body of local authority accountants, CIPFA compiles and publishes reports on local authority spending and finance.

Cm   Followed by a number, this indicates a 'Command Paper' presented to parliament. All reports of government departments are issued in this way and are numbered in simple chronology of publication.

Consolidated Fund   The Government's main account with the Bank of England. The largest part of central government expenditure is financed from this Fund and the Government's tax revenues and other current receipts are paid into it.

Control Total   The roughly £260 billion of government spending over which the government has some control, and so can plan with a degree of confidence. It excludes debt interest, cyclic social security, index-linked pension increases and accounting adjustments.

Council Tax   The means by which the majority of households contribute to the cost of services provided by local authorities. It replaced the Community Charge on 1 April 1993.

Current Expenditure   Public service pay and other current expenditure on goods and services. It includes direct expenditure on providing services, e.g. health or education, but not the operating costs of general government trading bodies, e.g. local authority ports.

Current prices   Refers to past expenditure figures that do not take into account the effects of any subsequent inflation, i.e. are quoted in money of the day.

DoE   Department of the Environment

DTI   Department of Trade and Industry

DfEE   Department for Education and Employment

DNH   Department of National Heritage

DoT   Department of Transport

EAGGF European Agricultural Guidance and Guarantee Fund. Across Europe, the Guarantee part funds CAP market support, and the smaller Guidance part funds structural changes in the way agriculture is carried out.

EC European Community. See Chapter 16.

Ecu European Currency Unit

ERDF European Regional Development Fund. See Chapter 16.

ESF European Social Fund. See Chapter 16.

EU European Union. See Chapter 16.

External Finance of Public Corporations Consists of financial support (lending, subsidies and grants) from central government for nationalised industries, trading funds and other public corporations, and their borrowing from commercial sources.

External Financing Limits (EFLs) The cash limits imposed by the Government on external finance.

FEFC Further Education Funding Council.

FSBR Financial Statement and Budget Report. Published on the day of the Budget, it provides a detailed analysis of the government's financial position, Medium Term Financial Strategy, and wider economic issues, as well as containing the Budget measures themselves.

General Government The central government and local authority sectors consolidated. See also Public Sector.

GGBR The General Government Borrowing Requirement. See Chapter 18.

GGE General Government Expenditure, the total spending by general government (qv). See Chapter 1.

GGE(X) GGE with certain items excluded, and often used in preference to the GGE, see above. GGE(X), with minor adjustments, is the definition of government expenditure used in this book. See Chapter 1.

Gross Domestic Product (GDP) (at market prices) The value of the goods and services produced by United Kingdom residents, including taxes on expenditure on both home produced and imported goods and services and the effect of subsidies. No deduction is made for depreciation of existing assets. Used as an index of the nation's wealth.

Gross National Product (GNP) GDP plus net income from abroad.

HC Followed by a number, this indicates a House of Commons paper for the session in question.

HEFC Higher Education Funding Council. There is a separate Council for each of England, Scotland and Wales.

LEA Local Education Authority.

Local Authorities Elected local councils, police authorities, fire and civil defence authorities, residuary bodies, passenger transport authorities and some other bodies controlled by councils jointly.

MoD Ministry of Defence.

NDPB Non-Departmental Public Body. Sometimes known as a quango.

Outturn, and Estimated Outturn Expenditure actually incurred or estimates made on the basis of partial information.

PCFC Polytechnics and Colleges Funding Council. Replaced by the HEFCs (qv) in 1993. See Chapter 4.

PFI The Private Finance Initiative, through which the private sector undertakes capital investment and charges the public sector for the use of facilities (hospitals, prisons, roads etc.). See Chapter 1.

Public Corporations Publicly owned trading bodies, usually statutory corporations, with a substantial degree of financial independence from central government and local authorities, including the powers to borrow and to maintain reserves. They include nationalised industries, trading funds and other public corporations.

Public Expenditure Survey (PES) The annual review of public expenditure plans undertaken by the Government.

PSBR The Public Sector Borrowing Requirement. See Chapter 18.

Public Sector Central government, local authorities and public corporations (qv). See also General Government.

Real; in Real Terms An expenditure that has been adjusted to remove the effects of inflation. Usually quoted with reference to the year for which the inflation adjustment has been made. For example: Defence spending in 1978-79 was £7.6 billion, but between then and now (1996-97) effective prices have increased by just over three times. So adjusting to today's money, the 1978-79 Defence spending was, *in real terms*, £23.4 billion (at 1996-97 prices). See also 'Current prices'.

Reserve Provides a margin for uncertainties and is intended to cover any future additions to spending, whether these result from policy changes, new initiatives, contingencies or revised estimates of the cost of a demand-led programme.

Revenue Support Grant (RSG) The major grant from central government to supplement local authorities' own finances. See Chapter 18.

RPI Retail Prices Index.

Running Costs The gross administrative costs of central government, including the pay of civil servants and all associated general administrative expenditure (including the costs of accommodation, travel, training etc). Includes the accruing superannuation liability costs for Civil Service staff under the Principal Civil Service Pension Scheme are included. Pensions in payment are excluded.

Subsidies Payments to trading concerns which reduce the selling prices below the factor cost of production. Examples include payments under the Beef Variable Premium Scheme and payments to housing revenue accounts.

Supply Expenditure Expenditure financed by money voted by Parliament in the Supply Estimates.

TECs Training and Enterprise Councils. See Chapter 5.

Trading Fund An agency (qv) not subject to central government running cost controls. Very similar to a public corporation (qv).

VAT Value Added Tax

Vote An individual Supply Estimate, see Supply Expenditure.

Note: A number of the above definitions have been drawn from the excellent glossary in the 1996 Scottish Office Report.

Index

179